Make Winning Bets In the "Lotto of Love"

THE LOVE LOTTO

PLUS

REVEALING PROFILES OF TOP
CELEBRITIES

BY

CELEBRITY LOVE GURU

MAMA LOVE

Email: themamalove@yahoo.com
Website: www.mamaloveconnect.com

© 2006 Mama Love

Note for Librarians: A cataloguing record for this book is available from Library and Archives
Canada at www.collectionscanada.ca/amicus/index-e.html
ISBN 1-4251-0614-5

Printed on paper with minimum 30% recycled fibre.
Trafford's print shop runs on "green energy" from solar, wind and other environmentally-friendly power sources.

TRAFFORD
PUBLISHING™
Offices in Canada, USA, Ireland and UK

Book sales for North America and international:
Trafford Publishing, 6E–2333 Government St.,
Victoria, BC V8T 4P4 CANADA
phone 250 383 6864 (toll-free 1 888 232 4444)
fax 250 383 6804; email to orders@trafford.com
Book sales in Europe:
Trafford Publishing (UK) Limited, 9 Park End Street, 2nd Floor
Oxford, UK OX1 1HH UNITED KINGDOM
phone +44 (0)1865 722 113 (local rate 0845 230 9601)
facsimile +44 (0)1865 722 868; info.uk@trafford.com
Order online at:
trafford.com/06-2372

10 9 8 7 6 5 4

CONTENTS

ABOUT THE AUTHOR

<u>MAMA LOVE</u>

Mama Love is an internationally renowned celebrity figure often billed as, "The Celebrity World's Favourite Love Guru, Numerologist & Psychic-Healer". She is recognized for her glamorous appearance, sense of humor, quick wit and "earthy" approach. Her Readings are known to be accurate, joyful and healing. She is always seen elegantly attired in jeweled gowns with matching turbans and a dazzling smile to match which attracts the media. Mama has been featured on numerous TV & radio shows as well as newspapers and magazines in the UK, Holland, Germany, South Africa, U.S.A., India, South America and Spain.

Mama Love confesses to being a hopeless romantic. She says, "As a Libra with the Life/Destiny Number, (LDN) 5 (the number of "Changes"), it is not unusual that I have spent a great part of my life in and out of love relationships. I have been married a few times and am looking forward to taking the "step" once again, because, (I'm not dead yet)! Now that I have matured, have learned many life-lessons and discovered the Romantic Numerology "key" to selecting a perfect match, I am convinced that my next husband will be my WINNING BET in the LOTTO OF LOVE.

Some persons may consider my romantic history as a demerit upon my character, but once they learn about the true natures of people in THE LOVE LOTTO, they will better understand me, themselves and others to become more lenient and forgiving in their judgements."

Mama's unique "Couples Readings" have garnered popularity with the public and the media. Cosmopolitan (UK) showed a three page feature on her doing theses unique Readings in March, 05. The application of her "Romantic Numerology" techniques bring out and accent the compatibility and harmony between couples. These Readings, explaining the couple's individual natures' to one another is Mama's light-hearted way of ironing out the small nits and creases (irritations) that often go unspoken in relationships. The core of any existing problem/s that may exist is quickly touched upon and smoothed over by the use of her sharp instinct and psychic-psychological knowledge and skills.

Mama Love has resided and travelled around the world as a "Citizen of the World" for the major part of her life in a quest for higher knowledge and experience. Viewed by many as a "Robin Hood" figure, she uses the high fees paid to her by her rich and famous clientele to go to the aid of the poor, needy and victims in disaster and war zones. She has frequently hitch hiked unaccompanied to dangerous battle areas to help and heal the victims in their time of need.

During these missions in war zones, she conducted private, candid interviews with some of the most illusive, notorious Leaders of the world. These healing missions and unique interviews gained her the honour of being listed for nomination for the Nobel Peace Prize, 06.

INTRODUCTION

WHAT IS "ROMANTIC NUMEROLOGY"

Basic Numerology is the study of numbers, similar to Astrology, the study of the planets.

Now, Mama Love introduces a romantic slant to Numerology that allows people to make better choices to insure more ultimate happiness in their love, sex and all other relationships. Her "Romantic Numerology" technique is a simple way of applying Numerology that is easy for all to follow. Using the numbers from one to nine, everyone with a basic knowledge of simple math can follow the instructions below to find their own and everybody's LDN (Life/Destiny Number).

The LDN is the KEY to discovering their own and others' basic characteristics, romantic and sexual natures, needs and destinies.

Mama Love guarantees that persons can be better, more accurately and quickly matched up romantically by their Life/Destiny (birth) Number, ("LDN"). If the reader follows her profiles of each "LDN", they will be more sure of finding their best love match/matches to "bet" on.

It's so simple! First, calculate your own "LDN" by following the instructions below. Then, look up your horoscopes to learn about your own nature and needs. After you learn about yourself, look up and study the other "LDN's" to find the one that you think would be the most compatible, harmonious and passionate match for you. Mama helps you make the right selections with her professional suggestions.

The instructions (see next page) of how to add the numbers together to find "LDN's" is simple. Using THE LOVE LOTTO guide will help the reader mend present relationships, save them from making future mistakes, losing precious time and suffering unnecessary grief!

In Numerology, each number vibrates a particular energy and colour in conjunction with the energy of the planet that rules it. These factors may not be visible to the naked eye, but play an important part in how people respond and harmonise to/with each other. The radiating energies from "LDN's" affect the psyche (more than you can imagine) and accurately highlight personalities and basic romantic and sexual natures.

The application of Mama's "Romantic Numerology" is much like a matchmaking "game". It is a proven method that promises everyone who follows it to finding themselves a WINNER in their next choices/bets for their future, "encounter", and/or most perfect love match.

NOTES:

Parents will find this book useful in learning and understanding their children's basic nature and needs. To understand natures' that may be contrary to, or compatible with yours, can be a big aide in knowing how to handle and guide your children objectively with <u>un-conditional</u> love.

THE LOVE LOTTO is also useful in looking up the natures' of your friends, associates and family so to understand and improve relationships with them.

YOU ONLY HAVE TO KNOW DATES OF BIRTHS TO FIND <u>LDN</u>'s, (Life/Destiny Numbers).

HOW TO PLAY THE LOVE LOTTO "GAME"
<u>FIRST CALCULATE THE LDN</u>

TO BE ABLE TO FIND YOUR OWN AND OTHERS PERSONAL LIFE/ DESTINY NUMBER (LDN) HOROSCOPES, MATCHES AND

FORECASTS

FOLLOW THE INSTRUCTIONS BELOW.

FIND YOUR LIFE/ DESTINY NUMBER (LDN)

<u>RULES:</u>

1. NUMBERS FROM 1 TO 9

2. CANCEL ALL ZEROS

3. REDUCE SUMS DOWN TO SINGLE DIGITS

ADD THE MONTH + DAY + YEAR OF BIRTH (DOB) THEN REDUCE THE SUM DOWN INTO A SINGLE DIGIT. SEE BELOW.

SAMPLE: THIS PERSONS D.O.B. IS: <u>2 MAY 1950</u>

| <u>DAY</u> | | <u>MONTH</u> | | <u>YEAR</u> |
| 2 | + | 5 | + | 19 + 50 = 76 |

REDUCE THE ABOVE SUM 76 DOWN TO A SINGLE DIGIT
$7+6 = 13$ $1+3 = 4$

THE ABOVE PERSONS' LDN IS **4**

NOW, CALCULATE YOUR OWN LDN ACCORDING TO YOUR DATE OF BIRTH, THE SAME WAY AS SHOWN ABOVE. FIND YOUR LDN HOROSCOPES, FORECASTS AND BEST MATCHES IN PART I. THEN, COMPARE YOUR OWN NATURE AND LIFE WITH THAT OF THE MANY CELEBRITIES DESCRIBED IN PART II.

PART I

CHAPTERS I THROUGH IX

INDEPTH LDN HOROSCOPES
LDN'S FROM 1 THOUGH 9

CHAPTER X

MONTHLY & YEARLY FORECASTS

CHAPTER XI

COMBINED LDN WITH SUN-SIGN HOROSCOPES

CHAPTER XII

LOVERS GUIDE & COMPATIBILITY CHART

CHAPTER I

INDEPTH LDN HOROSCOPES

LDN = (LIFE/DESTINY NUMBER)
1

RULING PLANET = <u>SUN</u>
KEY WORD = <u>LEADERSHIP</u>
COLOUR = <u>GOLD</u>

<u>OVERVIEW</u>

The LDN 1 signifies leadership and (Yang) energy derived from its' masculine ruling planet, the Sun. You as a LDN 1 are greatly influenced and motivated by its' dynamic energy. It is natural for you to feel that you must be the LEADER OF THE PACK. With your brilliant and dynamic presence, that should not be difficult for you to achieve. If you can't have your own way as the boss or leader, you prefer to do things on your own. You are a big hearted, generous person when things go your way and people obey your wishes. Even in your own home, you may have the tendency to take over as the "boss" of the house. Since you are very bright and have great ideas of how things should be done, being the boss is not such a bad thing but you must take care not to appear too bossy or commanding. MAMA LOVE suggests to her LDN 1's, to remember this: "IT'S NOT YOUR LYRICS THAT AFFECT OTHERS; IT IS THE SOUND OF YOUR MUSIC." LDN1's should try listening to the tone of their voice when asking others to do something, so they can reduce the tone of "command" to make it sound softer. You were born with a fiery, head-strong temperament and allow very little to stand in your way. In your enthusiasm you may over-extend yourself and be prone to projecting an excess of nervous energy. These are the times when you need to withdraw and conserve your resources in order to avoid total exhaustion. You may also become too impatient and domineering with others. Try to remember that everybody has the right to move at THEIR own pace and on THEIR own path. Yours, may not be the right one for them.

COLOUR INFLUENCE

The vibration of your colour Gold brings dynamic life-force energy to your. The shine and brilliance of the colour gives you a majestic aura that seems to place you above others. It makes you highly ambitious and gives you an insatiable need to reach your chosen goal whatever the cost. Gold is the colour of courage. Your nature demands you to be in the foreground, be noticed and drives you to take all the necessary steps to achieve this no matter how much courage it takes.

The Gold vibration creates your aura. It sends out the message that you are self-assertive, self-motivated with great passion.

CAREER

It is advisable for you to stay away from working for others. That would be very disabling for you because taking orders makes you cringe! If you choose to work within a large corporation, then you must try to hurry up your training and advance as quickly as possible so you can get to the position of managing your own department within its structure. It is of great importance to your nature for you to be the boss. If you are not the boss, your health can fail or you may take to drink and/or drugs to numb the inner pain you are feeling. Just remember, it is against your nature to be lesser than the first notch on the pole. All in all, the best career for you to pursue is a business of your own making.

LOVE AND SEX

You are a vigorous, demanding lover driven by a dynamic life-force energy. Sometimes your lovers may find you selfish or self-centred because the fulfilments of love and sex demands carry some degree of penetration into your partner's personal space. You may appear on those occasions, like "a bull in a china shop". You are extremely physical in your manifestation of love and sometimes feel that you must go through unnecessary motions in order to feel that you are "ok". You are motivated to take the lead and do it "your way" both in and out of the bed. This does not only apply to penetration, (the main factor in your sexuality). Your love is sensual and demanding. It's difficult for you to settle for plutonic relationships with those you are attracted to. You think that if it can't develop into a physical relationship, it is a waste of time. You can be generous and giving to someone that you are interested in as a conquest. Because love and sexuality are connected to physical fulfilment for you, this may hit you hard at an older age because you have it set in your psyche that "If it's not physical, it's not love".

LDN'S MOST COMPATIBLE WITH YOU ARE: 2, 3, 4 & 8

<u>CELEBRITIES WITH LDN 1</u>:

JIM CARREY, DANNY DEVITO, WYNONNA JUDD, DES O'CONNOR, KATIE HOLMES, TOM CRUISE, LIZ HURLEY, OZZY & SHARON OSBOURNE, GEORGE CLOONEY, DREW BARRYMORE, MARIAH CARY, DAVID LETTERMAN, SOPHIA LOREN, BRUCE SPRINGSTEEN, STING, DAVID CARRADINE, NICHOLAS CAGE, PRINCE HARRY, KATE WINSLET, DANNY DEVITO, SALLY FIELD

CHAPTER II

INDEPTH LDN HOROSCOPES

LDN = (LIFE/DESTINY NUMBER)

2

RULING PLANET = MOON
KEYWORD = PARTNERSHIP
COLOUR = SILVER

OVERVIEW

The LDN 2 signifies partnership and is charged with feminine (Yin) energy because it is ruled by the Moon, the feminine planet. Its characteristics are duality, partnerships, sensitivity and intuition. *You are sensitive, emotional, have a highly* developed imagination. Your main objective is to find peace and oneness through relationships. Since you are basically kind-hearted and like to please, you can appear to be "servile" sometimes but people soon learn that you can't be taken advantage of or pushed around. Although you are reserved by nature, that doesn't hinder you from standing up to others when you feel they are trying to take advantage of you. You are not a "born leader" and in fact, prefer to play a secondary role, yet at the same time, are very open to new ideas. You are a wonderful conversationalist, have good senses of humour and at times can be very witty. Your special gift is your highly developed intuition (ESP). Your only problem is your sometimes overly sensitive nature. An unpleasant look or comment is liable to offend you deeply and cause you to withdraw into an accusing blanket of silence. Then, you find it hard to forgive, even after some time. You won't argue with the person you feel has offended you; you simply withdraw and cut them off with a "silent treatment". By holding the hurt inside, you cause yourself and others needless pain and suffering because in most cases, they have no idea of what they did or said to hurt you so. You adjust to new things easily but if you're emotional or financial security is threatened, you are liable to become depressed, sometimes to the point of physical illness like ulcers and/or other digestive disorders. The cycle of the Moon influences your emotions as the Moon rules your LDN. Watch out for the influence of FULL MOONS!!

COLOUR INFLUENCE

Silver is the colour vibration that affects your life. Silver is a cool and lonely colour in that it is not in the normal colour spectrums and therefore often stands alone. It can make you appear mystical, but always very shiny and beautiful.

CAREER

You make the ideal business partner so long as you are left to do your part without constant interference. You have a co-operative nature and prefer to work WITH people although you have a need for independence as well. You are most particularly successful in careers that offer you the opportunity to serve people. Whether you are a man or a woman, you are most in tune (because of your ruling planet, the Moon) with dealing with women's needs, likes and dislikes. Selling residential real estate, for example is a possible career for you. Your intuition tells you what the woman will like and you are well aware that it is the woman who makes the final decision in the purchase of a home in most cases. You are very diplomatic so Politics is also a good career choice. You would know how to win elections by winning over the people with your diplomacy.

LOVE AND SEX

You are a faithful lover once you find love. Sometimes, you can purposely create obstacles in finding true love because you are so sensitive and afraid of trusting anyone with your heart. You are very giving and sensuous, especially around the full moon. Most LDN 2 males are known to be excellent lovers because their keen sense of intuition makes them sensitive to women's' needs and feelings. They never make untimely, awkward overtures. They can sometimes get into trouble with their spouses' or lovers' because females, in general, are magnetically attracted to LDN males and find them irresistible. (That's a hard thing for any male to always ignore.) The number 2 woman is feminine, sensuous, intuitive and responsive. All LDN 2's are romantic because they recognize that quality as a natural ingredient for love and/or lovemaking. The majority of LDN 2's are wonderful, sensitive, thoughtful and loyal spouses or lovers.

LDN'S MOST COMPATIBLE WITH YOU ARE 2, 4, 6 & 9

<u>CELEBRITIES WITH LDN 2:</u>

PRINCE WILLIAM, PRINCE CHARLES, PRINCE PHILLIP, CHRIS EVANS, MADONNA, BILL CLINTON, KATE MOSS, LUCY LUI, ED ASNER, RICHARD BURTON, KEVIN BACON, PARIS HILTON, JENNIFER ANISTON, MICHAEL JORDAN, RONALD REAGAN, ORLANDO BLOOM, MELANIE GRIFFITH, TONY BLAIR, DAVID BECKAM, GWYNETH PALTROW, DIANA ROSS

CHAPTER III

INDEPTH LDN HOROSCOPES

LDN = (LIFE/DESTINY NUMBER)

3

RULING PLANET = <u>JUPITER</u>
KEY WORD = <u>CREATIVITY</u>
COLOUR = <u>YELLOW</u>

OVERVIEW

The LDN 3 signifies creativity, joy and laughter. Jupiter, your ruling planet, is known as the planet of Luck so don't be surprised at your good luck in life. The dual vibrations of your colour yellow and your planet create a sunny, cheerful optimistic and strongly magnetic energy which makes you an extremely well liked and popular person. People are attracted to you. LDN 3's make successful politicians, public speakers, writers, designers, artists and media stars. You are a creative soul, full of clever, crafty and original ideas and are often one step ahead of everyone else. You don't have a malicious bone in your body and are non-critical. You will never grow up to be a grouchy, older person. The awareness of your own young child within you allows you and your inner child to live freely, openly and in harmony with your adult self. This is your main charm.

COLOUR INFLUENCE

The colour yellow creates an aura of happiness and optimism that touches everyone around you. Just as people are attracted to the sun, they are attracted to you. Yellow gives off a sweet, mellow vibration. People feel safe in its glow and feel cheered up if feeling low. You are protected by your aura of Yellow and it attracts good energies and good luck to you. If you go gambling, try wearing something yellow like a shirt or scarf just to re-enforce the lucky rays!

CAREER

With your magnetic personality and creative abilities you have a wide choice of careers. Performing in some sort of media such as cinema, TV, radio or theatre would be excellent for you and allow you the creative freedom your nature demands. Other No.3's can be successful artists, writers, designers, etc. You've "got it made" because of your magnetism. The public will always be attracted to you and your work. The choice is yours. You shouldn't face difficulties in any choice of career so long as YOU feel good with it. Most importantly, you need to EXPRESS yourself and have fun doing whatever you do.

LOVE AND SEX

Besides being an attractive looking person, you are emotional and participate in everything with a lot of exuberance. If you happen to fall in love with someone who is very restrained in revealing their feelings, you are bound to feel unhappy in that union. Your brand of love and sexuality is one that is expressed with a great deal of passionate and not without a light touch of "play". That makes you exciting and fun to be with. It is the lucky person who snags you as their love mate. So long as they keep you happy helping to keep the fires of love and fun burning, you will love them forever. You are destined to have good and even more importantly, a happy love-life. Your natural gift for projecting the aura of youth and brightness is big plus for you.

LDN'S MOST COMPATIBLE WITH YOU ARE 1, 3, 5 & 7

CELEBRITIES WITH LDN 3:

JOHN TRAVOLTA, BARBRA WALTERS, REESE WITHERSPOON, CELINE DION, JENNIFER LOPEZ, SADIE FROST, JAMES BROWN, CLAIR SWEENEY, LARA FLYNN BOYLE, PIERCE BROSNAN, ARNOLD SCHWARZENEGGER, DAVID DUCHOVNY, CARMEN DIAZ, JEFF BRIDGES, SHANIA TWAIN, FRANK SINATRA,

CHRISTINE AGUILERES, DIONNE WARWICK, ROD STEWART,

RICHARD MADELEY, STEVEN SEAGAL

CHAPTER IV

INDEPTH LDN HOROSCOPES

LDN = (LIFE/DESTINY NUMBER)

4

RULING PLANET = <u>SATURN</u>
KEYWORD = <u>WORK</u>
COLOUR = <u>INDIGO</u>

OVERVIEW

The LDN 4 represents the square and the cube; solidness, security and boundaries. You, as a LDN 4 person need to feel secure. You aim to build your life upon a firm foundation. Work is a normal, enjoyable part of your life, never an unavoidable "chore". You can become disoriented and restless if you are forced to leave or be distracted from your work for too long of a time. Yes, you enjoy holidays and good times out, but only for limited times. Saturn, your ruling planet has a strong influence on you to make your work the core of your life. In mythology, Saturn is depicted as the "old man" pounding steel. He is the one who repaired the other God's Chariots. He is always engrossed in his work therefore described as "the worker". Now don't start thinking that I am saying you are a boring person. I don't mean that. You can be quite sociable and amusing. You often find yourself in the role of BIG MAMA or PAPA because for as long as you can remember, you have been sought out by friends and family for advice and comfort. You know how to enjoy life and play (to a limit), but the line that divides you from being a "workaholic" is thin, so beware. You are solid as a rock and make a wonderful marital and business partner, friend and parent. You are extremely sincere in your affections.

COLOUR INFLUENCE

Your color Indigo creates a reclusive and serious aura around you. It throws out a vibration of solidness that gives people the feeling that they can always count on you to be there for them when they need you. It also can sometimes cause you to retreat and lose yourself in your work. When these spells occur, you lose awareness of others in your life. But underneath those occasional caves of darkness you retreat into, there is a very compassionate, caring, human being.

CAREER

Because you are practical, thorough, ambitious and a hard worker, you are good at any job you take on. If you are employed in a company, it will not take long for your position to be elevated once your excellent managerial skills are recognized. The administration aspects of a business are ideal for you. You are happy to work for others so long as they give you the opportunity to advance in their company. One of your pet peeves is poverty in the world, so your common sense and outstanding organizational skills can lead you to an executive position in a large charitable organization. You also can start up your own business and garner great success and earnings. You have a good instinct for what job would be best for you and can rise to great success through you own hard work. You are productive, decisive, punctual and a very reliable achiever, definitely NEVER a loser. In fact, you have good potential for becoming super wealthy.

LOVE AND SEX

In the beginning of a love relationship you are slow and thorough and are not easily seduced. You are a passionate and constant lover but before you bond with another, you have to be convinced that you are getting involved with the right person. Your approach is directed by both logic and emotion. Once you are sure he or she is the right one for you and make a commitment to the relationship, you hold no bars on displaying your love and affection. You're a conscientious parent and will always make sure your children are at a safe distance or asleep before you make love. You will seldom get caught up in moments of wild abandonment in your own home once you have children because you are too careful for that. You are not a dull person when away from your work place. You have a great sense of humour and your laughter is contagious. But mostly, you are a home-loving soul so although you may have a large circle of friends, you prefer the company of your family, lover or spouse. Once you emotionally commit yourself to someone, you become a strong, fundamental and passionate sexual partner, bringing to them a love that is balanced, sincere and long lasting.

LDN'S MOST COMPATIBLE WITH YOU ARE: 2, 4, 6 & 8

CELEBRITIES WITH LDN 4

DAILI LAMA, OPRAH WINFREY, BRAD PITT, MARILYN MANSON, NICOLE KIDMAN, SARAH FERGUSON, ELTON JOHN, WOODY ALLEN, JOHN KERRY, SEAN "P. DIDDY" COMBS, DEMI MOORE, BILL GATES, PAUL HOGAN, NICK LATCHY, PAUL McCARTNEY, LIONEL RICHIE, DENZEL WASHINGTON, DOLLY PARTON, KEVIN COSTNER, KEANU REEVES, TIM ROBBINS, RICHARD BRANSON, BONO, JADE JAGGER, CLINT EASTWOOD

CHAPTER V

INDEPTH LDN HOROSCOPES

LDN = (LIFE/DESTINY NUMBER)

5

RULING PLANET = <u>MERCURY</u>
KEYWORD = <u>CHANGES</u>
COLOUR = <u>ORANGE</u>

<u>OVERVIEW</u>

The LDN 5 signifies CHANGES and Mercurial energy. LDN 5's are known as courageous "Free Spirits" and "Non-Conformists". Until you fully understand your nature's as a number 5, you can live with a feeling of guilt for being "different" and always changing your locations, careers, ideas and sometimes, lovers. Know this: you should enjoy being "different" because you ARE "different". The number 5 in the middle of the numbers from 1 to 9 is an odd number, but it has its importance. Think of the: 5 senses, 5 clefs in music, 5 fingers, 5 toes, and the 5 pointed star, etc. Typical LDN 5's despise rules and regulations. If you are one of the few number 5s' that has become a conformist, you were probably controlled by your family and school as a child and made to feel guilty for starting different projects or courses without finishing them. How could your parents have understood that is the natural way for persons with the LDN 5 to learn and grow? It is not surprising if some of you try to keep your true nature in harness, away from the pressures of family, society and state. You will soon come to realize that being an extremely free spirit who INVITES changes to your life frightens your loved ones and can exile you from society. You may feel that people react to you as though you are from another planet! Well, maybe you are, but, that is an interesting trait not a bad one. The manner in which you take life's' changes in your stride and land on your feet to go on with the flow, is your way of growing and garnering knowledge. Know that your "oddness" has a purpose. Non-conformists like you were put here to jar people out of their robotic, controlled way of thinking. Most No.5's are married more than once, change jobs and careers frequently, love to travel, explore and try out residing in different countries on and off to garner more experience and knowledge. For you (to coin a phrase), "life is like a box of chocolates" Adventures and challenges are necessary for your growth. You certainly are an exciting and interesting person!

COLOUR INFLUENCE

Orange, the colour reflected from the planet Mercury represents communications and movement like the God Mercury who dashed across the skies with wings on his cap and heels in mythological tales. It is a vibrant colour and gives off an exciting vibration. Orange creates an aura of vibrant energy. People find you fascinating and love hearing your tales of adventure although most of them would never dare to attempt them themselves for the lack of courage. As a LDN 5, you were born as the Spiritual Warrior, the one who leaps into the dark abyss with blind faith.

CAREER

Don't expect to have only one career in your lifetime. You are too multi-talented and varied in your interests. Don't ever take on a nine-to-five job! No "ho-hum" routines for a number 5! You are very inventive, so like to dream up original schemes that haven't reached the market place yet. You could also enjoy a career in Communications or Journalism, (if it were as a "War correspondent"), for example. That would bring you the excitement and danger you're so attracted to.

LOVE AND SEX

When it comes to love and sex, your approach can sometimes be nervous and unpredictable. Your sexuality is strong but not the main issue for you in a relationship. COMMUNICATION is the key to your heart so you need a lover that you can talk with to exchange ideas and feelings. You are very magnetic and attract sexual advances in abundance. You can be extremely romantic and love the taste of adventure in and out of the bed. You are sometimes jealous and unfaithful like the type of "adventurers" written about in romantic novels. Maybe your unpredictable nature is what fascinates and attracts so many to you, while on the other hand, warns others to stay away. Perhaps they are afraid of being the moth to your flame. One thing your lovers can be certain of is that they will never ever be bored!

LDN'S MOST COMPATIBLE WITH YOU ARE 3, 5, 7 & 8

<u>CELEBRITIES WITH LDN 5:</u>

MICK JAGGER, TINA TURNER, BETTE MIDLER, SEAN PENN, JEREMY IRONS, CLAUDIA SCHIFFER, CATHERINE ZETA JONES, CARLY SIMON, MIKHAIL BARYSHNIKOFF, GEORGE MICHAEL, ANGELINA JOLIE, ANNA KOURNIKOVA, DON JOHNSON, LILY TOMLIN, LAUREN BACALL, SIMON COWELL, SEAN LENNON, BEYONCE KNOWLES, MARGARET THATCHER, KIRSTY ALLEY, SIENNA MILLER, SIGOURNEY WEAVER, GLORIA ESTAFAN, WILLY NELSON, JON BONJOVI, URSULA ANDRESS

CHAPTER VI

INDEPTH LDN HOROSCOPES

LDN = (LIFE/DESTINY NUMBER)
6

RULING PLANET = VENUS
KEY WORD = LOVE
COLOUR = PINK

OVERVIEW

The LDN 6 signifies love and romance. Your ruling planet Venus encases you in vibrations of love. Your nature is gentle and you are a home-loving soul who is always seeking balance and harmony. You totally emit the energy of love. The vibrations of your ruling, planet Venus the planet of love projects energy of safety, comfort and warmth. You have a great appreciate all forms of art and need to surround yourself with beauty. You're a very nurturing spirit marked as one who just can't say no. Sometimes you can feel that your good nature is being taken advantage of. At these moments, it is most difficult for you to put your foot down and say, "ENOUGH". Your entire being is dedicated to keeping love and harmony within the energies surrounding you. Your nature is most giving but you often feel that you do not receive your due in return because you confuse independence and self-love with selfishness.

COLOUR INFLUENCE

Your colour Pink encases you in a radiating glow of comfort, safety and warmth (love) which can be described as your "aura". It has gentle, romantic, healing love-energy, so it is advisable for you to decorate your home, (or at least your bedroom) in tones of rose and pink with objects of art and the sound of soft, romantic music to enhance your beauty and make you feel safe, comfortable and loving.

CAREER

It is said that LDN 6's make excellent teachers; not necessarily in schools, but as teachers of love and harmony. You need to work at something that will give vent to your creative taste and sense of balance and harmony. You would make an excellent designer, home decorator or artist. You find no problem working with a team if they are in harmony with your ideas and feelings. But you are best off working free-lance on your own so you can have the freedom to create beauty at your own pace. Acting could also be your forte. Actually, your selection of careers is limitless so long as it offers the harmony and balance you require making yourself and others feel good. Make sure, no matter what you do, that you are being nurtured and appreciated.

LOVE AND SEX

LDN 6's are the most romantic lovers of all. Ruled by Venus, you instinctively know how to love and create a romantic environment. It is no effort for you to be thoughtful and caring. Your lovemaking is romantic, sensual and gentle. You're so good at creating a romantic setting to welcome your lover/s. No doubt you "set the scene" with candles, soft music, satin sheets covered in rose petals and champagne chilling on the night table. Sometimes though you give so much love and are so giving that you forget yourself and your own needs. Your greatest weakness is giving BLIND LOVE. My special advice for you is this: Never, ever say the words, "I LOVE YOU", too soon! As a precaution I advise that you to wait until your lovers say it first at least <u>three</u> times. That way, you will be sure not to "jump the gun" and frighten them away. Give the other person time to assimilate their feelings before you rush into displaying your own deep emotions at the very start. Otherwise, you may make them feel pressured and smothered which may give them the urge to do a "runner"!

LDN'S MOST COMPATIBLE WITH YOU ARE: 2, 4, 6 & 9

CELEBRITIES WITH LDN 6:

HOWARD HUGHES, VANESSA REDGRAVE, JUSTIN TIMBERLAKE, CHERIE BLAIR, CHRISTIAN SLATER, MARTINE McCLUTCHSON, JOHN LENNON, MICHAEL JACKSON, ROSIE O'DONNELL, BILLY PIPER, LENNY KRAVITZ, LINDA RODSTADT, SYLVESTER STALLONE, JANE SEYMORE, JUDE LAW, KELSEY GRAMMER, JOANNE WOODWARD, BRUCE WILLIS, HEATHER LOCKLEAR, ROSANNA ARQUETTE, BEN AFFLICK, SALMA HAYEK, ROBERT DINERO, GERRI HALLIWELL, BRITNEY SPEARS, NICOLETTE SHERIDAN, GOLDIE HAWN, CALLISTA FLOCKHART, RICHARD DREYFUSS, DELTA GOODREM, GEORGE BUSH, LINDSAY LOHAN, S'INEAD CUSACK, KATE BOSWORTH

CHAPTER VII

INDEPTH LDN HOROSCOPES
LDN = (LIFE/DESTINY NUMBER)

7

RULING PLANET = URANUS
KEY WORD = SEEKING
COLOUR = PURPLE

OVERVIEW

The LDN 7 is that of the "Seeker". You are the most interesting of persons because you are the most interested in everything. Your mind is like a sponge. You can't help being curious and absorbing information to mull around in your mind in search of answers. The most important factor in your life is TRAVEL. Travelling is "food for your spirit" because searching for your own inner truth is the most important objective of your life. You are highly intelligent and diligent, yet also a free spirit. Extensive travel allows you to explore life and its mysteries. Some of you can be pessimistic, sarcastic and indifferent at times when you feel threatened by some unknown danger created by your imagination or felt by your intuition. Some LDN 7's are highly psychic as children and in advancing years have to make the choice of turning away or delving more deeply into this area of mysticism.

Generally speaking, neither money nor material comforts are your first priority so you should try to take care with your finances, at least enough to ensure your peace of mind and give you the freedom to EXPLORE.

COLOUR INFLUENCE

The colour Purple gives the vibrations of mysticism, the occult, and meditation. It gives you the aura of a "mystic" with a touch of the scientist added. The vibration of your colour can lead you in either direction. Purple attracts and draws many energies directly into your centre so sometimes you need to withdraw in order to assimilate new experiences and recharge your batteries.

CAREER

Generally speaking, you are a loner and find it hard to mix with others for any length of time, so it is advisable for you to choose a career that doesn't always require group effort. Something free-lance that you can do at home or on your computer when your travelling is best for you. No.7's frequently take the TEFL (teaching English as a foreign language) course, get their certificate; then spend years travelling around the world with the security of having a job when they need one, to keep them going and "on the road". Other LDN 7's find contentment as scientists or as writers. Others can be excellent alternative healers.

LOVE AND SEX

Since you are a deep thinker and a bit eccentric in nature, the average 9 to 5 person does not attract your attention. You seek someone who is deep and interesting like yourself to attract you with his or her "magical" aura. You are a gentle, attentive lover and grateful to have someone to share some of your thoughts and fill up the inner loneliness you often feel. But, you will still demand your own space once you form a firm relationship with someone. If they can't understand your need for that, it won't work out. You don't make demands on your lovers, but rather prefer to float into space with them in a dreamy-like manner. You are sensual but not overly sexual. They have to turn your mind on first if they want a response from your body. You seek ways of reaching higher, spiritual and mystical levels with your lovers. Becoming a "Tantric" lover could appeal to you.

LDN'S MOST COMPATIBLE WITH YOU ARE: 2, 3, 5, & 9

CELEBRITIES WITH LDN 7:

JOHN KENNEDY JR., ROGER MOORE,   MARILYN MONROE,

BRUCE LEE, JANET JACKSON, ETHAN HAWKE, MEL GIBSON, PRINCESS DIANA, LEONARDO DI CAPRIO, JULIA ROBERTS, BO DEREK, KEIFER SUTHERLAND, HUGH GRANT, ROGER MOORE, QUEEN ELIZABETH, JAMES WOOD, ELLE MAC-PHERSON, ERIC CLAPTON, AL PACINO, SADDAM HUSSEIN, RICHARD GERE, TANYA TUCKER, SUSAN SARANDON, JOHNNY DEPP, GUY RICHARDS, IMAN, ANTONIO BANDERAS, MICHAEL DOUGLAS, JESSIE WALLACE, JACK NICHOLSON, EMMA THOMPSON

CHAPTER VIII

INDEPTH LDN HOROSCOPES

LDN = (LIFE/DESTINY NUMBER)
8

RULING PLANET = <u>MARS</u>
KEY WORD = <u>POWER</u>
COLOUR = <u>RED</u>

OVERVIEW

The LDN 8 signifies prosperity and power. With Mars as your ruling planet, you can do anything you wish to do so if you set your mind to doing it. The vibrations of your ruling planet radiate power to the very core of you. It is your birthright and up to you if you choose to make use of it. You are strong, practical, bright, imaginative, intense, blessed as a multi-tasked person with a talent for organization. It is not difficult for you to run a conglomeration of corporations because your brain is equipped to organize your thought-patterns to deal with several things at one time. For example, if you are a housewife your home is surely run with the greatest efficiency yet you show no signs of it being an effort. People gladly do things for you because you are tactful in the way you give orders. You were blessed with a charming personality and that gets you what you want most of the time. However, beneath that charm lays a controlling, ambitious and materialistic person who seeks a high position and is usually very successful. Many politicians and World Leaders have the LDN 8, but most 8's find their success in the business world.

COLOUR INFLUENCE

The vibrations of the colour Red creates a "Warrior" aura about you. The Red energy is full of dynamic ambition mixed with an insatiable need to achieve your goal and then some. You are a great Warrior in the battlefields of the business world. You are like a red blaze charging to the top in your invincible Chariot. The colour Red that you reflect surrounds you in an aura that makes you appear extremely self-assertive, self-motivated and fiery in temperament, sending out the message that you won't allow anything to stand in your way.

CAREER

You are very efficient and a person of action which makes you suitable to head groups of combines. People feel your power and feel confident that you will make good use of it. They are impressed and allow you to take the lead, feeling that you will lead them to success. You are broad-mined and have excellent practical judgement. If you are young and just starting out in your career, don't be impatient, it will not be long before your attributes will be recognized, If you have the opportunity and means to start up a business of your own, don't hesitate. You will be SUCCESSFUL

LOVE AND SEX

You love and MAKE love with ardour and passionate. You know how to be tender at the same time and make your lovers' feel that they could never be loved or made love to better, than by you. Your problem in matters of love is that you always have so many things on your plate at one time; you can tend to neglect your love object by allowing the mobile to go off while you're making love. You also can blunder by leaving the bed directly afterwards to attend to some pressing business issue, leaving your lover on their own. It is against your nature, so virtually impossible to devote yourself to only one thing exclusively for any length of time and that includes romance and lovemaking.

LDN'S MOST COMPATIBLE WITH YOU ARE: 2, 4, 5 & 6

CELEBRITIES WITH LDN 8:

NAOMI CAMPBELL, TED TURNER, SHIRLEY BASSEY, ANNA NICHOL SMITH, JONATHAN ROSS, GEENA DAVIS, BEN STILLER, DIANE SAWYER, MAT DAMON, LIZ TAYLOR,

CINDY CRAWFORD, HALLI BERRY, MOHAMED ALI, OLIVER MARTINEZ, JOAN COLLINS, ENRIQUE INGLESIAS, MARTHA STEWART, RICHARD GERE, ARETHA FRANKLIN, SANDRA BULLOCK, TOMMY LEE JONES, LARRY HAGMAN, JAMES GANDOLFINI, ELVIS COSTELLO, PETER FALK, JANE FONDA, TATUM O'NEAL, JOSH LUCAS, JESSICA SIMPSON, NANCY REAGAN, AMANDA DONOHOE, GENE HACKMAN, WARREN BEATY, PAUL NEWMAN, TED DANSON, PENELOPE CRUZ

CHAPTER VIX

INDEPTH LDN HOROSCOPES

LDN = (LIFE/DESTINY NUMBER)
9

RULING PLANET= <u>NEPTUNE</u>
KEY WORD = <u>HUMANITARIAN</u>
COLOUR = <u>VIOLET</u>

<u>OVERVIEW</u>

The LDN 9 is a magical and holy number, unique in that when multiplied by any other number, the sum always reduces down to the single digit of 9 again. Most religious praying beads are strung in numbers that can be reduced down to the number 9, like 27, 108, or 99. The energy of the LDN 9 magnifies you as an "old soul" possessing wisdom that can astound others sometimes. That is because (if you believe in reincarnation), your soul has experienced many life time cycles and now being born as a No.9 this time, signifies this life-time as the end of a complete cycle for you. In this life-time you have the opportunity to recall all of the lessons you learned in previous lives to make this present one your life-time of "completion". You are not a "know-it-all" but you often get a gut feeling of understanding about most things. You may have frequent moments of past memory flashes of things that seem familiar to you, as though you experienced them before. That is because you have been through so many past lives. You have a keen sense of compassion for humanity. When you see the news about starving people, etc., it affects you deeply. Your ruling planet, Neptune casts an almost regal and spiritual aura about you. Life can be difficult for you at times because you experience alternative periods of successive victories and times of extreme difficulty and conflict. That is because your LDN 9 is the last and highest of the single digit numbers and signifies "spiritual achievement". It gives you the courage to come to the end; to let go of past experiences and make final corrections to all the errors you made over and over again throughout your prior life-times. Not an easy task, but very challenging.

COLOUR INFLUENCE

Violet is a spiritual colour. It creates an aura about you that indicates that you possess wisdom beyond your years. You seem to know the mysteries of the universe. Purple creates a regal and spiritual aura around you. People find it pleasurable and interesting to be in your company.

CAREER

You will excel in any type of work especially that which deals with people and feelings and/or the communication of feelings. Many LDN 9's make excellent painters, sculptors, writers, musicians, scientists, psychologists, social workers, teachers and doctors. You are able to work well with groups, but because you are such a creative dreamer but you enjoy and prefer working on your own.

LOVE AND SEX

You have a sensitive sexual nature. You are a very loyal lover or spouse if you are in love and most importantly, if you have firstly developed a deep <u>friendship</u> with them. Friendship is an important factor for the number 9 person to be able to commit totally. Normally, the number 9 person is not very demonstrative in displaying the emotion of love until they are completely immersed and bonded with their lover. For that reason, they can sometimes appear, at first, to be a bit "cool". (I would describe it as being more careful). It takes a LDN 9 some time to assimilate their feelings so to be sure that they making a correct and firm commitment. You are considerate of your partner/s needs and see them to be as important as your own, making you attentive and able to sort out any complaint or difficulty that may arise in the relationship.

LDN'S MOST COMPATIBLE WITH YOU ARE: 2, 6, 7 & 9

CELEBRITIES WITH LDN 9:

MAHATMA GANDHI, YOKO ONO,   RAY CHARLES, EMINEM,

IVANA TRUMP, CHRISTINA APPLEGATE, JADA PINKETT SMITH,

BRIDGET BARDOT, JENNIFER ELLISON, SHIRLEY MACLAINE,

KURT RUSSELL, LIZZY JAGGER, WARREN BEATY, LISA MARIE

PRESLEY, HARRISON FORD, CAMILLA PARKER JONES, RICKY

MARTIN,   ELVIS PRESLEY,   BARBARA STREISAND,   SHARON

STONE, CHER,   RENEE ZELWEGGER,   DUSTIN HOFFMAN,

CHARLENE TILTON, HEIDI KLUM, COURTNEY LOVE, PRINCESS

CAROLINE, TEA LEONI, JIM CARREY

CHAPTER X

YEARLY & MONTHLY FORECASTS

INSTRUCTIONS TO FIND YOUR YEARLY FORECASTS

PERSONAL YEARLY FORECASTS FOR
THE YEARS 2007 TO 20115 & more

YOU HAVE LEARNED TO FIND YOUR LDN ON THE PREVIOUS PAGES.

NOW, TO SELECT YOUR PERSONAL YEARLY READING/FORECAST

FOR THE YEAR 2007 AND THE FOLLOWING 8 YEARS TILL 2015,

SIMPLY ADD TOGETHER: YOUR <u>DAY</u> + <u>MONTH</u> OF BIRTH + <u>2007</u> (OR

WHATEVER YEAR YOU WISH TO KNOW ABOUT)

Add together the numbers 2 + 7 for 2007, remembering the rule of no

zeros in Numerology.

That gives you the sum of **9** for the year 2007 and **1** for 2008, etc.

<u>NOW ADD YOUR DAY & MONTH TO 9 TO FIND YOUR FIRST FORCAST FOR</u>

<u>2007</u>.

<u>EXAMPLE:</u> DATE OF BIRTH: DAY 5 + MONTH 10 = 15, 1 + 5 = **6**

6 + YEAR 2007 (9) = 15 THEN, 1 + 5 = **6**

THE ABOVE EXAMPLE: That person would select the number 6 forecast

below to find out their personal forecast for the year 2007. Begin with

the personal year number you get for the year 2007 then go to the following number (in the above case that would be number 7) for the personal forecast for 2007 and so on. When you finish the number 9 forecast; go to the forecast number 1 to continue your forecasts for more years to come.

EXAMPLE: If you get the same number 6 as the sample person above for the year 2007, you would begin to read forecast number 6 for your 2007 forecast. Then, continue with forecast number 7 to learn of your forecast for the year 2008 and so on.

TO FIND YOUR OWN YEARLY FORCASTS: FOLLOW THE DIRECTIONS ABOVE. YOU CAN DO THE SAME FOR FRIENDS AND FAMILY.

PERSONAL YEARLY FORECASTS

A No.1 YEAR is ruled by the Sun. This will be a dynamic year for you. You will find a new burst of energy and ideas to begin your projects with. You may be starting your own_company or business to find greater pleasure in being your own boss. This is the year for you to pluck up the courage to forge ahead with all of your new ideas and/or plans. Don't let them lie dormant too long. This is the year for you to TAKE ACTION. A good year to move into a new abode or even to a completely new area. This year you will feel like a newborn person with a pioneering spirit. A number one year is the year for new beginnings. GOOD LUCK!

A No.2 YEAR ruled by the Moon is a year to expect emotional highs and lows as the Moon goes through its cycle each month. If you are single, you will most likely find a love partner or enhance the relationship you are already in. New business partners may also appear or your current partnership/association could have the chance of finding new harmony. Try not to allow the cycle of the Moon draw you into too many emotional turmoils. This is the year for you to find your balance, harmony, romantic union, security and success.

A No.3 YEAR is ruled by Jupiter so you can relax more and have fun this year! Take more leisure time and let the "young child" within you rise up and take the lead. You will find yourself taking more time off from your work routine to PLAY. You will be able to get more involved in creative fun and will be able to take more spontaneous trips to the exciting places you've always dreamed of seeing. This number 3 year is a lucky year for you, a good year to try a little gambling. Don't be surprised if you win the lottery or something almost as good. DON'T WORRY THIS YEAR, BE HAPPY. GOOD LUCK!

A No.4 YEAR is ruled by Saturn so after the carefree times of last year number 3, you will be glad to get back into a more stable work time-table. You will find yourself laying plans to build up your life-security. This is the year you will work harder to save and/or invest your money in solid things like property. This is a good year to get married, settle down and begin a family. You won't be travelling too much this year, but will prefer to stay close to home and WORK. GOOD LUCK!

A No.5 YEAR is ruled by Mercury so be prepared for CHANGES in every area of your life this year. Be prepared to accept and meet the challenges to your life that this year will bring. You may suddenly decide to more to a new city or country and begin a completely new career and life. Your love relationship may change, as well as your career. You will feel like declaring your independence and freedom and fulfilling the dreams you have been harbouring for years. What ever changes you will make in you life this year, guaranteed, you won't be bored for a second! GOOD LUCK

A No.6 YEAR ruled by Venus will allow you to welcome the love, and harmony that the Number six brings. You will find and be filled with contentment. It will surely bring you heightened love/romantic experiences. Venus, who rules this year, will be hovering above you with Cupid near her poised to shoot his love arrows into your heart.

This is an excellent year for healing emotional wounds. Last year was a hectic one for you, so now you can look forward to more harmony and balance in your life. It is a good year to redecorate your home to create a more relaxing, romantic and harmonious atmosphere because you will be entertaining quite a lot. GOOD LUCK!

A No.7 YEAR ruled by Uranus is a most interesting year. You will find yourself wanting to quench your thirst for knowledge. You will feel a need to feed your "higher-self" and search for your inner truth. This will lead you to travelling, reading, attending lectures, etc. You will meet new, interesting people. They may inspire you to seek more information about things you may have been curious about for many years as well as new subjects you will come across. You will be able to solve a lot of the mysteries of life this year for this is the year of DISCOVERY. GOOD LUCK!

A No.8 YEAR ruled by Mars is a year of power and prosperity. You will find it quite easy to get things accomplished with an ease that will amaze you. You will be able to take on all of the projects that interest you and never feel too busy to take on one or two more and cope with your heavy load with ease. Your inner strength will rise up to help you organize your life and aim for a position at the top of the heap. Don't be surprise to be offered a higher position in your field of work.

This will occur because others will sense your ability to direct and organize. This is the year of abundance so feel free to grab at success. GOOD LUCK!

A No.9 YEAR is ruled by Neptune. The number nine is the last number in modern numerology and represents completion. This year signifies the end of a cycle in your life. It is the year to "cleanse", wind things up; close all open circles and to let go of all old pain, grudges and anger so that you may explore the higher mysteries of life and within yourself. You will be taking interest in the more spiritual aspects of life this year; perhaps travelling to remote places in search for universal knowledge. You will make more time for doing philanthropic deeds like starting up or working for a good cause that you believe will help the Unfortunates of this world. Clean your pallet this year. Next year will be a number one year for you with new beginnings.

BEST MARRIAGE YEARS FOR EACH LDN

LDN 1	1, 4, 5, 7	LDN 8	1, 2, 6, 8
LDN 2	1, 5, 6, 8	LDN 9	2, 3, 6, 7
LDN 3	3, 6, 7, 9		
LDN 4	1, 4, 7, 8		
LDN 5	2, 5, 7, 9		

LDN 6   1, 3, 6, 9

LDN 7   1, 2, 4, 8

MONTHLY FORECASTS

The following monthly predictions are general. If you would like to make them more personal, compare the number of the month to that of your LDN. That month will be the strongest and most successful for you because the same planet rules the month as rules your LDN.

JANUARY This is a number 1 month ruled by the Sun, a time for new beginnings. This could mean a new job or career, a new romance, a new health regime or diet, a new home or new objectives, etc. The Sun planet will fuel you with it's' energies to enable you to begin new projects with confidence. Feel safe in being determined to forge forward with your plans. The Sun's energy will make you feel like taking the lead in situations where you may have usually been more docile. Don't be surprised at your incredible surge of high-energy and self-confidence this month.

FEBRUARY This is a number 2 month ruled by the Moon. Be prepared to go through emotional highs and lows this month, especially around the full moon. You will reflect upon the projects you began with zest and confidence last month and sort through them with more thought. The Moon's influence touches your intuition and will guide you to reflect upon your decisions of the month before. You may or may not change your plans slightly but can count on coming up with better ways of approaching them. Keep your eyes and heart open. You may form a new business partnership and/or find new love or better the relationship you already have this month.

MARCH   This is a number 3 month ruled by Jupiter. Jupiter is known as the planet of good luck. Things will begin to bloom and go your way. It's a good month be more daring and take chances you normally wouldn't. Your chances of acquiring success, winning money, gaining popularity and being invited out a lot are pretty good this month. It is a month to party and enjoy life. If you live in a cold climate, you may get the urge to holiday in a sunny spot. You will feel like going to parties and clubs more frequently than normal. This is a month to dance, sing and make merry!!!

APRIL   A number 4 month ruled by Saturn. This may be a bit of a duller time because it is the month for slowing down your merry-making of last month and settling into a more serious work routine. A lot will be accomplished in your work place. It is a good month to concentrate on building a firm foundation for your life. It is also a good month to firm up your relationships and pay more attention to family, love and business partners/ associates.

MAY   This is a number 5 month ruled by Mercury. Be prepared for some excitement! This is a month of "changes". A good time for travelling, exploring, possibly changing your place of residence or even switching careers. Mercury rules communications so it is a good time to be around those who have unconventional, exciting views and ideas. You will find yourself wanting to meet new people in distant lands or to learn a new language, etc.

JUNE This is a number 6 month ruled by Venus. This month is filled with promises of love and romance. It is no coincidence that there are more weddings booked for June than any other month of the year. It is filled with flocks of birds, bees and flowers casting lovely scents in the air that create romantic urges in most everyone. Expect romance this month. You can be pretty sure of finding it. It is also a good month to be nice to yourself and try to put your life into more balance and harmony. Spread your love energy around this month and it will be sure to make its way back to you.

JULY   This is a number 7 month, ruled by the Uranus. This month fills you with a yearning to seek, travel and explore. It is the month to take holidays in most zones of the world because the children are on school break, most city businesses not geared for summer merry-making, slow down. and in most places, the weather beckons us to the sea side or cool mountains. If you can't or don't go away, this is an ideal time to browse the book stores for interesting material to read or to enrol in a course to learn more of something you've always been interested in. Your mind is in the "exploration mode" this month.

AUGUST This is a number **8** month, ruled by the red planet, Mars. Although you may still be enjoying your summer holidays. you will find yourself organizing your plans of action for the future in the back of your mind. This is the month to reflect on your life and make plans for your future.   You will crave to be more in control of yourself and everything around you.   It's the time to put more order in, your life, and your career so you can feel that you are in charge. You will be enhanced with a feeling of power to do anything you want to do. It will affect your love and sex life too. Expect to be more active than usual!!

SEPTEMBER This is a number **9** month ruled by Neptune. The number nine is the number of completion. It is the time to bring thoughts and experiences of the past months to orderly conclusions so to be able to begin anew with fresh views of your future. This month can initiate new beginnings in your mind. September brings the changing of season, getting back to school or work routines and generally has an atmosphere of preparation. You will feel a renewed energy after the summer months. You should have a feeling of being refreshed and ready to begin a new season.

OCTOBER This is another number 1 month ruled by the Sun, but has a different vibration than January. This is a time for new beginnings but more interior ones than exterior. You will feel energetic and enthusiastic about your plans. It is a good month for starting anew in your relationships with others. You will be feeling the need for more harmony and love in those relationships. It is also a good time to initiate new "research" actions. October can also bring your social life back into the light. Most people are back from their holidays and have spent last month reorganizing their lives, so now are ready to resume their social life.

NOVEMBER This is another number 2 month ruled by the Moon that can be a bit "blah" because it's near the end of the year and people tend to be storing up their energy for the festivities of the next month. This is a time for developing the seeds that you have sown in September and October. People with gentle and magnanimous characters will find joy in everything this month, even the small but frequent expenses that will occur. Most things that happen now are related to that which is close to you such as home, spouse, parents, children, subordinates and friends.

DECEMBER This is another number 3 month ruled by Jupiter. It is expected to be filled with joy and social activities. Lots of new contacts will be made to keep you busy developing them. You will spend more money than usual in carrying out personal activities such as entertaining yourself and others at parties, buying presents, dining out, receptions, corporate and holiday festivities. The air is filled with an energy of abandonment filled with a bit of nostalgia because another year is coming to an end. Inwardly, you will have hopeful and optimistic feelings that the coming new year will bear more fruit and happiness than the last. It is the month for reunions with old friends and family, so rejoice!!

(AN EXTRA BIT OF INFORMATION)
DAYS AND THE PLANETS THAT RULE THEM

SUNDAY   SUN

MONDAY   MOON

TUESDAY   MARS

WEDNESDAY   MERCURY

THURSDAY   JUPITER

FRIDAY   VENUS

SATURDAY   SATURN

CHAPTER XI

COMBINED LDN & SUN-SIGN HOROSCOPES
LDN 1 THROUGH LDN 9
(WITH EA CH OF THE 12 SUN-SIGNS)

LDN 1 / ARIES

This combination of your LDN Sun-Fire with the Fire of your Sun-sign is quite a dynamic duo! You may run people down like a lawn mower gone wild if you are not careful. You should realize how dynamic and over-powering your nature can be and try to tone it down at first meetings, especially at job interviews. The best advice I can give an LDN 1 / Aries is to be aware that the sound of your music will/can soften your lyrics.

Sexually, WOW! You can break more than one bed in your lifetime! You need a lover who can deal with and enjoy your powerful, dynamic, not always terribly romantic love-making "style". You are highly sexed and demand lots of it. You don't always have the patience to "romance" your partner/s because you want it when you want it but you can delight the partner who is your ideal match.

LDN 1 / TAURUS

This is an interesting combo. As a Taurus, your earthy and romantic approach is appealing. You are an attractive person and can charm people with your Venus smile and ways. In business matters, you excel because you are both aggressive, decisive and at the same time, sensible and practical. You don't mind working hard for what you want. In fact, you must be careful not to push yourself too much. Beware of becoming a "workaholic".

Sexually, you are aggressive, passionate and diligent. The LDN 1 part of your nature urges you to take the lead and display dynamic passion. When your Taurus nature takes over, it introduces more romance into the sex act which is pleasing to your lover. You have a big, lusty and loving sexual appetite. Your sexual demands are frequent but, most of the time, basic. It is not your nature to explore too many variations on the theme because you are frequently too preoccupied and exhausted by your demanding work schedule, anyway. You tend to be possessive about your loved ones and can get jealous at times. The Sun and Venus combination is both dynamic and romantic.

<u>LDN 1 / GEMINI</u>   This is an interesting combination of Mercury and Sun. The direct approach of the LDN 1 part of you combines with the fluctuating, ever-changing, free spirited nature of the Mercurial

Gemini to make an interesting person. Your Sun energy heats up the Mercury so you may find yourself not being able to stay interested in a job or career for too long of a time. Your life will be an interesting one and you can expect a decent degree of success.

Sexually, you actively enjoy yourself in bed. Gemini's are generally very good-looking people so you will appeal to the opposite sex and probably get what you want most of the time which please your LDN 1 nature. You attract the opposite sex and know how to "go for it". You have the pick of the litter. As a marital partner you will always "take care of business" in the bed department, but you may not be the most faithful lover in the Universe because your nature craves diversion.

LDN 1 / CANCER

Here we have a more complicated combination. Your Sun-sign, Cancer has a watery influence that can conflict with your LDN Fire. The Sun that rules your LDN is masculine in nature. The Moon that rules your Sun- sign is feminine. This may influence you to fluctuate from having a masculine approach and reaction then a feminine one. Your inner conflicts are sometimes great. Beware of the full Moons. That is the time of greatest confusion and conflict for you. The full Moon brings out your feminine nature and makes you feel especially sensitive and vulnerable. Your dual nature is fascinating and makes you attractive to many. You are pretty much of a "home body" and devoted to your family.

Sexually, you can take the dual approaches of the male and the female at the same time. This can be a big "turn on" to many. One moment, you may be assertive and aggressive and the next, more sensuous and passive.

LDN 1 / LEO

Hurry! Somebody reach for the water! This is a dynamite, combination of natures. Fire and Fire! Don't be surprised if some people tend to cower in your presence especially if they work under you. You are exciting to be around but hard to take for any length of time. You can easily exhaust people with your headstrong and demanding energy. I don't mean to say that you are an unpopular person. On the contrary, your peers find you exciting and clever, (but only in small doses). Many find your dynamic, bright energy and enthusiasm quite attractive.

Sexually, you can be like a keg of dynamite in bed which can be great if you don't blast off too quickly. It may be difficult for you to think about your partners' feelings when you are in the "throws of passion", but try. You will be more welcomed the next time, if you do. Your love-making is own way.)

LDN 1 / VIRGO

Now, here we have an earthy LDN 1. You are a down to earth person, very neat in your ways. You have very precise ideas of how you want things done. For this reason, you can be a "pain in the neck for persons who are working under or with you. Try not to drive them crazy about every small detail of order and cleanliness that you insist on. Your physical presence is immaculate. You always look well groomed. But even though you may be a "neat freak", everyone who takes the time to look, can see the sparkle in your eyes!

Sexually, you are a dynamic lover as all LDN 1's are, but you are a little more careful. It can be either way, depending on how tightly your Virgo nature is tied to your LDN 1. You are considerate as you like to be considered and wouldn't think of entering the bed until you were bathed and in the case of a male LDN, shaved. You generally don't go for any "kinky" sex, but you may be convinced to try a new position once in a while. The sheets, you and your lover are clean and fresh now, so get on with.

LDN 1 / LIBRA

You are a more easy-going LDN 1. Your Libra, (Venus) qualities soften the harder approach your LDN nature brings you to. You concentrate more on being charming as you give orders. When you are aware of slipping into the demanding, bossy LDN 1 mode, you quickly tone it down to a more amiable level. You are generally a well liked person. Your good looks are a great asset!

Sexually, one could guess that you manage to give your lover/s the best of both your natures, (dynamic and romantic). You are quite sensual and can reach moments of high romance.

LDN 1 / SCORPIO

You are wonderfully successful in business or any career you have. You easily figure people out and know how to deal with them. You also can spot an untrue person instantly and will avoid having any kind of dealings with them. You are well liked and respected but people don't get too close to you at first in fear that they may cross you and make you angry. No one likes the thought of that Scorpio sting!

Sexually, you are a terrific lover if and when you trust your lover/s. You can be vicious if you feel that your lover has been unfaithful. Promiscuous sex is not "up your alley/street" so much. You prefer a deep, intense relationship although you are extremely sexual and

CRAVE sexual encounters. You are pretty much centred on your sex life.

LDN 1 / SAGITTARIUS

Here we have Fire with Fire but the flames are not as "devouring' as other Fire with Fire combinations. You are exciting and certainly very interesting. You love to travel and learn about what life is all about. It may be difficult for you to find others that are as interesting or that can keep up with you and all your interests. Nothing slips past you. You always have your eyes wide open. You are a sociable person and enjoy being in the company and conversing with others.

Sexually you need a fiery but not quite so dynamic a lover as you are or you could burn each other (and the bed)! You are an adventurer and enjoy sex in unusual places, not always just in the bed

LDN 1 / CAPRICORN

Your LDN 1 ruled by the Sun's forceful energy can sometimes overwhelm and conflict with the nature of your earth sign. Capricorns' like to tread carefully and take their time making decisions. LDN 1's, in general, usually don't hesitate. They just get on with it. The Sun's energy force drives them forward towards their goal with blind determination but Capricorns' are more careful so you may feel a pull from your dual natures.

Sexually, you have a healthy, lusty appetite most of the time. The only time you may disappoint your lover/s is when your Capricorn nature dominates and draws you into a shell where your immediate desire is to be withdrawn into yourself. Some, not all Capricorns' can tend to be "voyeurs". Those who are may encourage their sex partner to make love with someone else or take part in orgies so they can watch. Capricorns' are not too interested in the "higher", spiritual aspects of sex, but rather in the basic earthy side of it. This goes hand in hand with your LDN 1 nature that leads you to satisfaction through direct action.

LDN 1 / AQUARIUS

Your LDN 1 nature leads you to take direct action with no advice or control. Your Aquarian energy is more airy and creative with a wise approach. You are confronted with the combined forces of Fire and Air. The Aquarian side of your nature is rather cool and thoughtful, sometimes to a calculating level that helps you get what you want. It also prevents you from stepping on too many toes including your own and guides you to getting your way without appearing to be too much of a bossy LDN 1.

Sexually you are aggressive and delight in taking the lead as a LDN 1. Your Aquarius nature, on the other hand, saves the day by creating a good line of communication between you and your lover, so that the sex act holds another element other than "just doing it". It is important for you to establish a deep friendship with your lover/s first. That is how you become the best lover you can be. You also enjoy a bit of fantasy in your love-making on some occasions.

LDN 1 / PISCES

As a Pisces, you could sometimes have the tendency to wallow in darker corners of your mind, but the bright Sun, the planet LDN 1 is ruled by saves the day and draws you out of the darkness. Piscean persons are basically kind hearted and know compassion which softens the bossy, demanding, sometimes selfish aspects of a number 1 who is depicted as, The "Leader of The Pack." All in all, this combination makes the Pisces side stronger and more determined and the LDN 1 side a little softer, hopefully to reach a happy medium and create success and happiness.

Sexually, you are a more compassionate and affectionate lover than the average LDN 1 when and if the Pisces side of your nature is allowed to come forward. Most times, it ends up being a passive/aggressive "happening", which could be found quite interesting and satisfying to your lover/s.

LDN 2 WITH SUN-SIGNS

LDN 2 / ARIES

Moon and Fire is this combination. This makes you gentle and sensitive on one hand and assertive and aggressive on the other. You are successful in business or any career you pursue. Your fiery energy combined with your kind, diplomatic manners get you ahead.

Sexually, you are active with a very strong sex drive. Sometimes you can actually be romantic, while other times you are just passionate and direct with the urge to take what you want when you want it. When wooing someone, you can be very winning and attractively convincing.

LDN 2 / TAURUS

Here is a very earthy LDN 2. It is a good combination of Water and Earth. You will always have money because you are a hard worker and know how to manage things. People like you because you are a loyal friend who doesn't let anyone down. You are always there for them. When you get hurt or angry, your aggressive Taurus nature can spring up to surprise some people.

Sexually, if a male, you are depicted as the "Bull", so take it from there! You are a strong lover and go for who or what you want; yet you have the sensitivity and sensuality as a LDN 2 which is appreciated. Both male and females with this combination are sensitive but very lusty lovers and can be quite possessive.

LDN 2 / GEMINI

Your Gemini sign saves the day for you by lifting you out of the emotional turmoil's you sometimes fall into as a LDN 2. Your Gemini influence makes you creative, an artist of some kind. In fact, you are gifted in many different areas. Whatever you choose to do, it will be successful because you will be loyal to your commitment most of the time. That depends on how strong the changeable Gemini influence is in your nature. Your LDN 2 nature makes you a loyal friend, attentive to their needs, but you have to be treated gently because you are easily offended.

Sexually, you are intuitive and sensual. You are generally a faithful lover, but that Gemini "thing' can make you flirty. You like to laugh and "play" with your lovers in and out of the bed. That is the "young child" in you that escapes whenever he or she can.

LDN 2 / CANCER

Here we have the case of a double Moon (Water) influence in the same person. That is not easy to contend with. It causes you to take life very seriously. You are a pleasant and caring person but your bouts with emotional despair are hard on you. You are at your best when you are near or on the water, so living by the sea or lake or river is a good idea. On the other hand, living on a boat would be perfect!!!

Sexually, your lovemaking can be like the gentle ripples of the sea and sometimes really dynamic and exciting like the big waves of an ocean. Either way, you are a sensuous, wonderful lover when you are not retreating into one of your sullen LDN 2 "spells".

LDN 2 / LEO

An interesting combination of Sun and Moon influences. It can sometimes be an actual battle of the masculine and the feminine. Your Leo side (Fire) wants to shine and strut and can do so if your LDN 2 sign (Water) doesn't put out your fire too often. This combo of natures makes for an interesting person. Your intuitive, considerate LDN 2 can soften your aggressive, forceful Leo characteristics and turn you into a well balanced and very well liked person.

Sexually, things can go well either way. Your sex partner/s gets the best of both the feminine, (Moon) and masculine (Sun) with your combined nature. You can be aggressive or passive or both at the same time! You are a combination of the Yin and Yang so having sex with you always promises surprises!

LDN 2 / VIRGO

These two signs blend together very nicely. You are a neat, hard working, honest person. Your appearance is always immaculate and you are very careful with people's feelings. In the work place, you are well liked and respected. Socially, you do very well and have lots of loyal friends because you, yourself are a loyal one.

Sexually, you are a thoughtful, sensitive lover. Your overtures are slow and rather shy at first, until you are sure of reciprocation. Then, once you're sure of your lover/s affections, you go straight on and take 'care of businesses with passion, thoughtfulness and care.

LDN 2 / LIBRA

You are a good looking, sociable person. You love to enjoy life to its fullest. Your sensitivity and intuitiveness as an LDN 2 combined with your charm and good looks as a Libra makes for a popular person. Sometimes your flirty Libra nature is misunderstood so your more sensitive LDN 2 side of your nature bears the pain.

Sexually, the first thing that comes to mind is the thought, "Fly me to the Moon!" This is the best way to describe you as a lover. You are sensitive, romantic, fun-loving, and considerate, all in all, wonderful lover!

LDN 2 / SCORPIO

"Water, Water, don't let me drown"! That's what you and others may think sometimes because you are a very intense, sensitive, intuitive, emotional person. The torment you sometimes feel inside is induced by your own emotional response to things. You are kind and considerate to people in hopes that they will be the same to/with you.

Sexually is the department where you excel. If someone is lucky to get you as a lover and be able to cope with your extremely sensitive nature out of the bed, they will receive the greatest of pleasure from you in the bed. You don't often disappoint your lovers.

LDN 2 / SAGITTERIUS

Here we have a well-balanced number 2. You are a person with many varied interests. This makes you a very interesting person. You enjoy travelling and exploring, which you do with heightened pleasure. You are sociable and well liked. People are always interested to hear about the new things you have discovered about life, places, etc.

Sexually, you take joy in making love but are not normally the promiscuous type. You prefer having only one partner to share your life and your body with. You are thoughtful, affectionate and quite dynamic in your lovemaking at times.

LDN 2 / CAPRICORN

Your combination shows a complex nature. Both aspects when they come together can produce moodiness. No, you are not ALWAYS moody! You are very ambitious and strive to get to the top of the mountain of success. You are a loyal friend, but very sensitive so your friends have to be careful not to offend you. When and if that situation occurs, you get more hurt than angry and you close the door to whoever offends you. They go off feeling miserable and bewildered and you're left behind to suffer inwardly.

Sexually, you are a wonderful lover. Your nature is one that is very giving. The influence of your Moon sign, a feminine planet, guides you to make the right moves at the right time. The Capricorn side of you can take you away from your partner for days when you escape into your own inward space. Be careful not to cut your lovers off as if they don't exist. They should know that it is worth understanding your moods because when you return to the space you left them in, you are very passionate and attentive. You can only hope that your lover/s understand and don't leave you in that interim, feeling neglected and abandoned.

LDN 2 / AQUARIUS

Water is the element that rules your LDN. Aquarius is an Air sign, so you are a mixture of Air and Water. Neither one does much for the other. You can appear to be a rather cold Person, a bit aloof but in reality, you're just up in the air, dreaming away. You have a lot of compassion and are intuitive, so you can spot when someone is feeling low and you try to console or counsel him or her.

Sexually, you are quite sexy in a dreamy sort of way. You can display a lot of emotion and may even enjoy a bit of fantasy in your lovemaking. Role-playing can be a part of your sexual "play".

LDN 2 / PISCES

You are an intense mixture of the Water with Water. A good but complicated combination. You are extremely emotional, always fluctuating between feeling happy and a bit depressed. You are an extremely sweet and caring person but you have a dark side to your nature that you rarely show to others. You would do well in a career that caters to women. You have great empathy to their nature.

Sexually, you can be a fabulous lover. You are sensuous, intuitive to what your partner likes and needs and your approach is more towards pleasing than taking pleasure for yourself. There are few whom you could / would not satisfy.

LDN 3 WITH SUN-SIGNS

LDN 3 / ARIES

Whopa! You are a lively person full of beans! You have a high-pitched personality and nature which may attract many and keep others at bay.   You are creative and possess the drive and determination to get ahead in life. Sometimes, you can be a bit self-centred, caring only for you're on needs.

Sexually, you are a lively and creative lover but sometimes can be a little over bearing and demanding. You also can display feelings of jealousy when you feel that your lover is not focused entirely on you, you, and you.

LDN 3 / TAURUS

Your combined nature can be a bit like a seesaw but most times keeps its balance. As a LDN 3 you're lively and playful and let your inner child rise up but your Taurus nature doesn't allow you to "fly" too far away from the earth. That part of you is sensible and "takes care of business" at hand. You have an excellent business "sense" and will do well when mixed with your creative nature.

Sexually, if you allow both of your signs to work together, you should be a satisfying lover. You can fill your lover/s with joy and give them ultimate satisfaction. You are strong and firm in your actions.

LDN 3 / GEMINI

You possess a great blend of natures. Light, airy and creative, that's what you are. You are fun to be around, therefore, are quite popular. Your looks and personality are magnetic. You can keep heads spinning (even your own) because you are usually involved with many things at the same time. You are attractive, magnetic and a creative "communicator", so could do well in the performing arts.

Sexually, you don't have any problems attracting the opposite sex. But, you can't be counted on to be a one on one person for too long of a time. You need variety in your life so; can become bored with someone easily if they are not as creative and lively as you. Even when you are madly in love, it's difficult for you to stay faithful, though, perhaps, in your heart, you would like to.

LDN 3 /CANCER

The watery Cancer side of your nature is happily counter-parted by the light and airy qualities of your LDN 3 Air sign. As a Cancer, you are devoted to your family and make sure that your creative endeavours don't keep you too far from the hearth. You are a sensitive, thoughtful person and that makes you well liked by most everybody.

Sexually, you are a sensuous lover who always tries to please. Your lovemaking is wholesome and intense for the most part, but can get adventurous at times because of the creative and playful side of your nature.

LDN 3 / LEO

You are a lively "Combo"! With all the FLASH and glamour of a Leo combined with the creativity and good looks of a LDN 3, you need never be in doubt of attracting attention. This is an extreme case of the (LDN 3) Air blowing the (Leo) Fire to great proportions! I don't see where you can go wrong. You can have a very successful career in any creative field you choose. Your good luck number 3 sign makes your success in becoming rich and (possibly) famous a pretty sure thing.

Sexually, you can wow anyone with your "pizzazz". Not a big, only a HUGE bed, (with a bottle of champagne chilling by its side) is for you! Satin sheets are a must, preferably gold or red in color. Everything you do is on a "grandioso" scale so you can be counted on to give your lovers a "grandioso" good time!

LDN 3 / VIRGO

You should do very well in business and in life generally because you bring your creative nature down to your sensible Virgo level. The mixture is a good one. While you maintain your creative initiatives, you develop them into a blend that is workable. You are popular because both sides of your nature shine through. Your earthy and meticulous approach is softened and lightened up by your lively, child-like LDN 3 qualities.

Sexually, you can be either direct, without much need for intricate foreplay or your number 3 nature can take over and demand the later to an extreme. Your playful LDN 3 nature keeps you from being a bit of a bore and too much of a "goodie, goodie" in bed.

LDN 3 / LIBRA

Happy, fun, fun, that's what you are most of the time. You are very attractive, lucky, creative, amusing and most likely; successful and popular. Things go your way most of the time. This allows you to display the best part of your two natures combined. Your charm and beauty get you most things you want. Remember, your LDN 3 is the number of luck ruled by Jupiter, the planet and the God. The God Jupiter is often called the "Lord of Luck". Mixed with your Venus, you can't lose.

Sexually, you excel as a lover and "seducer", but can't be counted on to remain faithful all the time. In some cases you may be so to someone you love very much, but they may not believe you are because you are a ruthless flirt! You can't help it. It is your nature to flirt and tease.

LDN 3 / SCORPIO

You are a loyal, fun, creative person and a joy to be around until you feel someone crosses you. In that case, you can become a dangerous foe. But, your "sting" is more than balanced by your jovial and magnetic personality. You do well in your career because you are a mixture of light-heartedness and intense concentration. You know what you want and usually get it by your wit, cunning and calculated moves.

Sexually, you are intense, dynamic, intriguing and passionate with a dash of fun mixed in. You can give your lover/s a bit of everything. Being an airy LDN 3, you are less intense and jealous than most Scorpios'.

LDN 3 / CAPRICORN

You have conflicting natures but they can find a way to work together. The LDN 3 side of you is creative and happy-go-lucky. Your earthy Capricorn side pulls you to the ground but shouldn't take the fun out of your life. Your Capricorn sign with its good business sense, hard working nature and ambition combined with the creativity of your LDN 3, can lead you to success.

Sexually, you are creative, fun loving and ardent when you are in not hidden away in your "inner sanctuary". Sometimes, you bewilder and cause hurt to your sex mate when you retreat into yourself and leave them feeling like they're on their own in bed. You're just not there! (in body perhaps but not in mind)

LDN 3 / AQUARIUS

As a LDN 3 you are naturally a lucky person. If you get the opportunity to become rich, you will show compassion for humanity and want to give some charitable offerings to the poor & needy. You are a fun person to be around and your quality of understanding attracts people to you.

Sexually, you can be "heavenly" when your inner child pops out to take the lead. Your partner may be in for some fun surprises that will delight them. When you are in love, you are quite active sexually. You enjoy creative, playful and sensuous sex with an accent on fun-foreplay.

LDN 3 / PISCES

Lucky, fun, creative, sensitive and sweet are the words that can describe you. You are normally quite sympathetic and kind to others, except when your inner volcano explodes. Then, watch out everybody! The inner turmoil that your Pisces sign creates within u can overcome your normal creative and fun loving nature.

Sexually, all depends on whether your luck is running high or low. When your life is running smoothly, you are a great lover, but when you're having financial or other problems, you're not interested at all, preferring to lurk in the darkness of your inner sanctum.

LDN 4 WITH SUN-SIGNS

LDN 4 / ARIES

"Solid as a rock", that's what your LDN 4 makes you. You do not wish to move far from the spot you choose or have chosen as your domain. You will stay there and defend it with your fiery Mars nature and be content to build up your life/career brick by brick until you reach success. Success comes to you because you are willing to work hard, without wavering. You are more likely to have your own business or self-run career than to work for others.

Sexually, you are a satisfying lover. You make love with passion and purpose. You're a caring partner as an LDN 4, but sometimes your Aries nature can lead you to being a bit demanding and self centred.

LDN 4 TAURUS

You are the most "grounded" of all the combined natures. Nothing, but nothing can sway you from your career or your family. People sense that you are an "always there" person and they can depend on you. That makes you popular and well loved by all. Sort of a "Big Daddy" or "Big Mama".

Sexually, you are true to your nature being consciences and passionate in your lovemaking. Even when overworked, you are able to be aroused and enjoy a good "toss in the hay".

LDN 4 / GEMINI

Contrary to the above combination of signs, you are more likely to try several different careers or jobs before you find one you really feel comfortable in. Even then, you may switch careers later in your life. Your Gemini energy gifts you with many creative talents so there are a variety of things you could be successful with. It is your nature as a "twin" sign to fluctuate a bit when you are young, but your LDN 4 nature eventually grabs hold with time and influences you to stick with one thing long enough to earn you success.

Sexually, you find it more difficult than the average LDN 4 to remain completely faithful to one person. You will be LOYAL, but not always FAITHFUL. In other words, if you are married you won't leave your mate for another but may "fool around" sometimes. You are a good lover and a bit more "creative" in bed than the average LDN 4.

LDN 4 / CANCER

Ho, ho, your chosen match should know what they're getting when they choose you because you will never let them go. You are very sensitive and tend to hold grudges. You can tend to cling, are faithful and expect the same from all your family and friends. You are a hard worker but family is your first and foremost concern. You generally become the Matriarch, Patriarch or Manager your entire family and arrange all the family reunions, etc. You may even put yourself in charge of creating or keeping the family tree up to date.

Sexually, you are most faithful and demand the same from your lover/s. You can be a wonderful, "dreamy" kind of lover when your Cancer nature comes to the fore. Your LDN 4 nature is sexually dynamic and passionate. This combo of natures can be a terrific and extremely exciting in bed. You will never let your love match down if they are careful not to offend you.

LDN 4 / LEO

You are a LDN 4 with more "flair" than most. You are not just a hard worker, you have to be the boss and run whatever business/career you may have. You are driven to success by not only your nature as a LDN 4 but also by your Leo ego and lust for the luxurious "high" life. You are rather bossy, so not always the most popular person when your Leo nature rises up. But, your loved ones know you will always be there to help or advise them if/when they have problems.

Sexually, you are a passionate and demanding lover when you are young. You flirt a bit but normally will stick to one partner once you find one you can "command" to be faithful. As you grow older and more involved in your career and drive to succeed, you may have to occasionally be reminded that your bed is more than just a place to sleep in.

LDN 4 / VIRGO

Your combination of natures makes you like a double-edged LDN 4. You are more likely to become a "workaholic" than the most of the other Number 4's. Once you choose what you want to do/become, you don't waver for an instance. You are a double earth sign that makes you devoted to your work whether it is in business or as a homemaker. You are a devoted parent and_partner, eager to make sure that all those beneath your wings are happy and content.

Sexually, your combined nature is much the same in bed as the above description. You have your moments of great passion even when you are exhausted from the days work. Sex is an important ingredient in nurturing your body and spirit. It confirms your love both given and received.

LDN 4 / LIBRA

Here we have a bit of a conflict. Your LDN 4 wants to keep your nose to the ground but your airy Libra instincts create the urge to fly around like a butterfly having fun. It will take someone with this combination a longer time to settle down into a long-term career or committed relationship. You will always be successful because you know how to make money. You like to "play around" and socialize but you will postpone it till you are sure that you have the extra funds to do so.

Sexually, by nature you seek one lover but can't stop your flirty nature from coming forward even when you are with the one you love. You will never stray but will always flirt. In bed, you are ardent, lusty and romantic. What more could anyone ask for?

LDN 4 / SCORPIO

This is a combination to be careful with if someone should have any treachery in their heart. They won't be left off easy if they do something to anger or lead you to mistrust them. You are a very ambitious person who won't be content with anything but total success in whatever you do. So long as no one "crosses" you, you will be the most loyal of friends.

Sexually, you are both sexual and sensuous but tend to look for solid relationships more than one night stands. Your love is intense and fervent. Your lovers will never feel neglected or forgotten in the bed with you.

LDN 4 / SAGITTARIUS

You are a LDN 4 who likes to explore beyond the basic life you create for yourself. You have many different interests but can stick to one thing for success if you have to. The fiery side of your nature can sometimes scorch the earthy side. If you manage to balance your energies, you should find happiness and do well. You are likeable and an interesting person so don't find it difficult to gain popularity.

Sexually, you are equally earthy and fiery in the bed. That makes for a "hot time" for all. You don't disappoint your partner/s unless you've burned yourself out and need some time and space to get your energies aligned and strong again. So, your lovers will have to understand that sometimes you may seem disinterested in having sex, but it is not your fault. If given time to rest up you will come back to their attention with new gusto.

LDN 4 / CAPRICORN

You are a grounded person bearing the nature of two combined Earth signs. You are reliable, a good friend and an excellent parent. You're pleasant to be around but are usually too busy with your work to take much time out for socializing. Saturn with Saturn, you are very ambitious and will go the whole route to get to the top in your field.

Sexually, you are a strong lover when you're in the mood. Your Capricorn nature can lead you to going inward. During those times you can neglect your lover's needs for days or weeks at a time. You have a little secret desire that is hard to express to your lovers if you feel they may have a negative response. That is the "Voyeur" part of your nature.

LDN 4 / AQUARIUS

Some of you can do well in a scientific or humanitarian oriented job or career. Many with this combination enjoy studying things that are "out of this world" but others can be consumed by their great compassion for humanity and prefer to direct their energies toward making things better for those in need. You are attractive and well liked but you're not that interested in society and a very active social life. You prefer to live in a world of your own making but despite this, you usually find success because of your LDN 4 nature, which drives you to be successful and make money.

Sexually, you are a good, strong lover, sometimes very earthy in your approach. Other times, you can be "far out" and try new positions and ways that you read about. Your lover has to be ready and open to a bit of "exploration" in the bed.

LDN 4 / PISCES

Sometimes you tend to take life too seriously. You're earthy, practical LDN 4 nature can be flooded over by your watery Pisces nature. You would be wise to make a conscious effort to try to keep a balance. You are a hard worker like all number 4's but you can suffer from bouts of depressions and self doubt. Your friends try to help you out of these moments because they know you to be a sweet, carrying person.

Sexually, you are a good lover when you are in balance. You accommodate your lover/s when you feel they desire sexual attention but you're not the one who initiates it when your Pisces nature is taking the lead. Your LDN 4 nature (when in the foreground) gives you an earthy, passionate approach to sex.

LDN 5 / WITH SUN-SIGNS

LDN 5 / ARIES

You are a dynamic duo. The changeable nature of the number 5 is combined with the aggressive assertiveness of your Aries nature can be hard for some more conservative people to cope with. There is nothing shy about you. You are a sociable and aggressively exciting person. You enjoy handling several projects at the same time. When you travel around and make new friends, they never forget you!

Sexually, you are a whirlwind of energy. You excite and satisfy your lovers, but always make sure you are satisfied first and foremost. Your Aries nature is a bit self-centred. You could have a big ego, so watch it.

LDN 5 / TAURUS

Your Sun-sign Taurus slows you down just enough so people can keep up with you. As a LDN 5 you're apt to spin like a top a lot of the time, so it is good for you to have the Taurus nature to ground you. You will do better in business than other LDN 5's because you will be able to stick to one thing for a longer time and even see the project out to the very end. You are a dependable person and generally, well liked.

Sexually, you are a firm and faithful lover but you can have the tendency to be possessive and jealous. Your Taurus nature is a lusty one so your lover/s will not complain about not being "attended" to.

LDN 5 / GEMINI

Wow! Here we have the mixture of 50% Mercury with 50% Mercury. That, as you can see, adds up to 100% Mercury! You're certainly an interesting and exciting, creative person (most likely an artist), but may be hard for others to keep up with where you are and what you are doing at any particular moment. You attract everyone around you with your' good looks, creative skills and non-critical personality. You also may frighten people who are very "grounded". They don't trust you.

Sexually, you can guess from the above description that you can be a whirlwind of sexual energy in the bed. Generally, you are very highly sexed and delight in having a variety of partners. This is natural for you, as the "Communicator". You can please them all with no problem.

LDN 5 / CANCER

You are a much calmer LDN 5. You are more likely to want to be near or upon water. The ideal life for you would be to live on a boat. That way, you could be on the water you are so much a part of and at the same time gives vent to your adventurous number 5 natures by traveling the world as an "adventurer". This would be the perfect solution for the dual sides of your natures. The family is very important to you so that may limit you to staying on the ground and sadly, in one place more than your LDN 5 nature would like to. In either case, you are a good and loyal friend or family person. Your sensitive nature makes you become offended, sometimes, too easily. Try to forgive more easily.

Sexually, your sexual desire is based more on your emotions. You prefer to be emotionally involved with your lover/s. You don't find the one night too satisfying and as you get older, you can be loyal to one person without a problem.

LDN 5 / LEO

A dynamic duo of energies! Mercury and the Sun can make a very "hot" combination of natures. You are dynamic, bossy, exciting and hard to be around in close proximity for any length of time. But, you are well liked and admired for your "dashing" ways, glamorous approach and success in accomplishing so many things in one lifetime.

Sexually, you delight your lovers with your luxurious tastes and passion. Even if you are not rich, you manage to have the champagne and strawberries chilling by the bed. Nothing but satin sheets for you! You are at your best when the "scene" is set properly. Then, you are more at ease to continue the scenario with passionate lust and variety of themes to keep your lover/s fascinated and satisfied.

LDN 5 / VIRGO

The Virgo side of you calms down the adventurous side of your LDN 5 nature. Instead of zooming around the world seeking new experiences as other LDN 5's may do, you tend to stay closer to home. You are more likely to conform to the society's rules where you live instead of being the typical LDN 5 non conformist. You prefer to live a more peaceful, simple life, working and building and structuring a secure life style.

Sexually, you are a willing and able lover although you can be a bit reserved about exploring alternative ways or "tricks" in the bed. The ole 'classic" with a few but not too many varieties is good for you, being that you're not a great adventurer. If your lover/s coax you to try different things, you can be convinced and willing to give it a go even if you feel a bit awkward at first.

LDN 5 / LIBRA

You are the last word in non-conformity! You are a "Rebel" (with or without a cause). You refuse to be under the rule of anybody or any institution and you possess the courage to do things your own way. I think the song; "I Do It My Way" was written about a LDN 5/LIBRA. You are well liked because you are a whirlwind of Mercurial energy and excite. You are very attractive will be a hopeless flirt till the day you die!

Sexually, you are very romantic and although you like variety and change in your life, you like your sexual encounters to be motivated by love and romance. One-night stands are not your thing. You like to ensure that your lovers love you, even if it is only for that moment. You are loyal and monogamous, but it can't be guaranteed for how long of a time. It is your nature to change partners more frequently than most. It's not unusual for you to marry several times.

LDN 5 / SORPIO

You are an interesting combination of energies and natures. As most LDN 5's, you are a free Spirit and a non-conformist. You are a loyal friend to those who are loyal to you. You air of Scorpio mystic adds to you attractiveness. Any business or career venture you try will be successful if you want it to be.

Sexually, you can often be both mystical and magical in bed. Your love and lovemaking is very emotional and intense. You expect your lover/s to be faithful to you but can't promise the same. You can't resist trying out your sexual prowess and attractiveness with the opposite sex. It may be innocent play for you, but could upset a faithful lover and make them lose their trust in you.

LDN 5 / SAGITTARIUS

Oh boy! Here we have a real "road runner". It's hard to keep two combined natures like yours tied down to one place, job or person. It's easy for you to make money and survive so you are not obsessed about having security. You know it will always be there because it is within you. If you do become/are rich, you will have homes in several different places.

Sexually, you are passionate, loving and sometimes a bit demanding in the bed, but again, you are dealing with your LDN 5 nature and we all know by now that it is hard to keep you "down on only one farm". You need variety and have the skills to easily get it. If you are young, you're likely to settle down to one person once you are matured.

LDN 5 / CAPRICORN

Your Capricorn nature is to be a hard worker. You can get lost in your work and don't have time to gallop around like a typical LDN 5. You are more settled in your nature and like staying in one place so you can accomplish your tasks. Your LDN 5 nature is usually a bit curbed by the way you sort of live inside of your own head and imagination. You are well liked and respected. People take you more seriously than they do most LDN 5s'.

Sexually, you can become invisible in the bed sometimes when you are living in your own inner world. Your lover/s has to get use to being ignored some times. It's not that you don't love or desire them; it's just that you get lost in your own thoughts. What may wake you up is to find another person in bed with you and your lover. That would perk your interest as the voyeur that you can sometimes be. That trait too, is a part of your secret inner world.

LDN 5 / AQUARIUS

You're a blend of similar natures. Aquarian's like to search for the truth and explore life so your LDN 5 nature of Changes is a compatible blend. You like flying around the world to see, explore and acquire new friends and "Gurus" all over the world. People like you because you are exciting yet gentle, kind and understanding. You are a good listener and like to soak up as much knowledge as you can.

Sexually, you are a sensuous, sometimes romantic lover. But your sex drive does not always take priority. You like to know a person well before you take them as a lover. Creating a friendship first, is one of your basic needs. You like a bit of fantasy and a lot of foreplay in the bed. Once someone "hooks" your attention and heart, you have no problem making them feel very loved and satisfied in and out of the bed.

LDN 5 / PISCES

Your Mercury, LDN 5 nature leads you to the water where you can explore the depths of it and life like the Pisces fish you are. Thanks to the LDN 5 part of your nature, you don't get lost in the deep waters for too long. Your Mercury influence keeps you occupied with communicating with the world. You're a sweet, considerate person and people enjoy and benefit from your friendship.

Sexually, you are considerate and caring in the bed. Sometimes your passion can rise to high proportions, but that doesn't occur all the time. You are capable of being very faithful to one love because you have an inner insecurity and fear of being abandoned. Back to the depths of the sea you would go if that happened to you!

LDN 6 WITH SUN-SIGNS

LDN 6 / ARIES

Your Aries ruling planet, Mars makes you a more dynamic LDN 6 than most. But, the planet Venus that rules your LDN plays a role in softening your Mars warrior qualities. The two completely opposite sides of your nature may confuse some persons. Sometimes they don't know whether to love you or hate you. You're exciting, creative and good-looking. Success is yours and if it doesn't come to you easily, you will MAKE it happen because you are ambitious and aggressive.

Sexually, you are interested in sex and active as a lover. Your LDN 6 side craves romance whereas your Aries side is content with a good sexual encounter, romantic or not. You have the qualities to make a lover very happy. For the most part, you are faithful to the person you love.

LDN 6 / TAURUS

Both your Sun-sign and LDN are ruled by Venus so there is no lack of romance in your nature. Beauty, balance and harmony are the keys to your inner being. You need to surround yourself with all three things. Your taste in music, art and antiques is exquisite. You would be very successful as a decorator or an antique or art dealer. Anything that is connected to beauty and fine arts is a perfect avenue for you to pursue. Of course, you are a well-liked person. You are good-looking and always dress with good taste.

Sexually, you are both romantic and passionate. The most important thing for you is to be assured that your lover is well attended to and satisfied. That is not a difficult task for you. Just be careful not to be too overbearing and show signs of insecurity that may manifest into signs of possessiveness and/or jealous.

LDN 6 / GEMINI

You are a loving person with a bit of "pizzazz". With your combined nature, you could do well as an art dealer who seeks new works from artists all over the world. You have a good feeling for the Arts and your Mercury influence urges you to travel as one of the "Communicators" of the art world. No matter what career you choose, you will do your work with good taste. You are popular and have an active social life because you are good looking, exciting and pleasant to have around.

Sexually, you don't take a "back seat" to anyone. You have a strong sex drive and throw a lot of romance into it, being a number 6. You tend to fall in love often and passionately.

LDN 6 / CANCER

The combination of Air and Water that makes up your nature doesn't create the most exciting person, but you are pleasant and easy to be around. You are a real "home body". Your home, family and the ones you love are the centers of your life and you are willing to make sacrifices for them, if necessary. Interior decorating could be successful career for you. You have a flair for it and know how to create a setting to make clients feel comfortable in their homes.

Sexually, your lover/s should appreciate your romantic and loving nature and should realize that you need as much affection as you give. Sometimes, you may be a bit overbearing in displaying your love. That may make your lover/s feel "trapped", but that depends on whether your natures are compatible or not.

LDN 6 / LEO

With this combination of Air and Fire, you not only NEED love and affection, you DEMAND it. Your Leo nature urges you to make enough money so you can ideally, live in the sumptuous style you crave. Your home is adorned with a lavish collection of art and antiques to please yourself and dazzle viewers. You enjoy entertaining and "holding court" in your home like a King or Queen. You are a generous host/hostess and people enjoy your gracious company.

Sexually, you take the lead most of the time. Your sense of romance combined with passion will fulfill your lover/s if he or she cares for you and responds with mutual feelings of love. Love and affection is the key to your heart and sexual responses.

LDN 6 / VIRGO

The Earth and Air combined influences of your Sun-sign and your LDN 6 give you a grounded and hard working nature. You are meticulous in everything you do. You need things to be orderly and beautiful at the same time. You are a loving, honest and caring person, so you attract friends who appreciate your qualities.

Sexually, your nature is to nurture and make sure that your lover is well attended to in the bed. You display affection with generosity but your performance is not so demonstrative as to overwhelm. You have an almost shy quality that makes you a good but conservative lover. Normally, most persons with this combined nature would not so comfortable when/if a lover wants to introduce something a bit "kinky" but that is not the rule. Some of you could also go the other way and delight in a bit of "kinkiness".

LDN 6 / LIBRA

A double Venus like you is the epitome of love and romance. You LIVE for luxuries, harmony, love and romance. You are very good looking and appealing to the opposite sex. Basically, you seek love, but that is sometimes difficult to interpret because you are such a helpless flirt. You are the grand "seducer". You are most happy working in a creative field that allows you to free-lance.

Sexually, the bed is where you feel most at home. You love being in love and excel as a lover using the ingredients of romance, passion and "special effects" to arouse and delight your lover/s. You nature prompts you to make the encounter/s as romantic as possible and setting "the scene" with candle light, flower petals on satin sheets, perfume in the air (as well as on your body) and we mustn't forget, the soft music playing in the background.

LDN 6 / SCORPIO

You are a loving person possessing a mysterious aspect. You are more cautious in exposing the vulnerable, LDN 6 side of your nature. This creates fascination for people and they feel attracted to you because of that quality. You are a true friend, loyal and caring. Rejection is the one thing you don't take too easily.

Sexually, you are a "giver". You display your love in abundance and with powerful lust. Sex is where you excel and demonstrate your true nature and feelings towards your lover/lovers. Pity the one who crosses you by lying and/or being unfaithful. They would certainly have to face your Scorpio sting!

LDN 6 / SAGITTARIUS

Yours is an interesting combination of natures. You have the LDN 6 qualities of being a loving and harmonious person mixed with a dash of excitement because of your fiery Sagittarius sun-sign. The mixture of Fire and Air always make for excitement. There is never a dull moment around you. You always have interesting things to talk about and discuss with people because you are well read and traveled. You are never dull.

Sexually, you can't and don't fail. You are full of love and find various ways of displaying that in the bed. Your lover/s won't have much to complain about. You can give them the best of both; the affection and the ACTION!

LDN 6 / CAPRICORN

As a Capricorn LDN 6, you are more cautious in displaying your feelings. You don't rush into relationships too quickly to guard against any possible rejection. But once you feel "safe" with that person, you are a loving and loyal friend. You have good taste in art and music and could possibly be involved as an artist in either field. You take your work seriously and strive to do well and achieve success.

Sexually, you can be a wonderful lover. You have to be in the mood though and not too deeply immersed in the private place in your mind you frequently escape to. That can leave other person at a loss for understanding what has happened to make you seem so disinterested. The Capricorn side of your nature is what draws you into a private world of your own, at times. But if your number 6 nature comes to the fore, you soon return to the moment very aware of your lover/s, to their and your own needs with great affection and passion.

LDN 6 / AQUARIUS

You are an exceptionally gracious and thoughtful person. That makes you well thought of by the society in which you live. You are likely to do a lot of charity work because you are a humanitarian. Your loving and caring nature, along with your beauty and appreciation for the arts can all be accredited to your popularity.

Sexually, the LDN 6 side of your nature is always eager to love and be loved. The sex doesn't play as important a part as the "love making". The Aquarian part of you is usually there to fulfill your lovers' needs as well, but not always so eagerly. This causes a fluctuation in your behavior in the bed. This could prove interesting, add a bit of intrigue and be an interesting challenge to your lover/s.

LDN 6 / PISCES

Your combined nature is a wonderful blend. You are sweet natured, loving and romantic. People are drawn to your charms and small glints of mystery. Your best nature comes forth if and when you are near or on water. It is easy to imagine the female with your combined natures as being a lovely Mermaid and the male, a friendly Dolphin.

Sexually, you "swim" through lovemaking with the grace of a romantic, dreamy lover. Your basic incentive is to make LOVE. You are only "unavailable to participate when you slip into the depths of the dark sea, (of your mind).

LDN 7 / WITH SUN-SIGNS

LDN 7 / ARIES

LDN 7 is known to be the "Seeker". When combined with the nature of a Warrior like Aries, you are not always so open to accepting much of information you garner, as fact. You are fiery and willful and sometimes think you are a "know-it-all". You possess a storage of information and are interesting to listen to but the influence of your planet Mars dominates and can sometimes make you appear self-centered and hard to approach. People could feel that you would be hard to get along with.

Sexually, you redeem yourself and prove to be a good lover. You possess the Fire as well as the Air of mystery and exploration to create excitement and passion. Just don't place your lover/s needs second to yours.

LDN 7 / TAURUS

Yours is a romantic and mystical combination. Your combined natures create an interesting person who has their feet on the ground and their head up in the clouds. If you become interested in one particular subject, instead of just dreaming about it, you may turn it into a viable way to make a good living with it.

Sexually, your Venus nature makes you a romantic and passionate lover and along with your LDN 7 nature, add dashes of mysticism and exploration to the "event". You can either have a lese faire or possessive attitude in your intimate relationships. That depends on which side of your nature rears its head.

LDN 7 / GEMINI

There's not much that can keep you down on the ground. Uranus and Mercury combined, points to a life of travel and excitement to explore as much of the world and the secrets of life as you possibly can. Your friends become accustomed to seeing you at intervals between your journeys. Your energy is very attractive to everyone wherever you are. If you don't or haven't followed the urgings of your nature, you could be a frustrated person but then, you may find an outlet in the practice of some expressive art form to "save the day".

Sexually, you can create feelings of "magic" in the bed. You enchant and delight, but your lover/s shouldn't expect total faithfulness. You're too much of a curious "explorer".

LDN 7 / CANCER

Here is a complex union of natures. It is masculine and feminine, scientific and dreamy. The best way a LDN 7 / Cancer can vent their dual desires is to perhaps buy a yacht and explore the world by sea with your family in tow. That would satisfy all your desires and make you feel complete. You need to stay close to home and at the same time need to feel free to explore.

Sexually, you are more loving than passionate, not to say that you possess no passion. Of course, you have moments of great passion, but that is not your most forward initiative to making love. You try to reach a spiritual level in your romantic union/s. This gives you a sense of security in the relationship. You can be faithful if you find the right person.

LDN 7 / LEO

You would be more likely to explore great dynasties or be a collector of expensive, rare antiques. Things of Grande appearance appeal to you as you are attracted to glamorous and ornate, gold-crusted objects. Your energy is dynamic and you try to make discoveries that will "rock the world". You are a more exciting type of explorer. When you travel, you like to do it in style. First class only, please!

Sexually, you display great passion but are not very romantic in your approach. You can tend to be too direct and not that considerate of you lover/s feelings all the time. You always have to take the lead and feel awkward in playing the passive role.

LDN 7 / VIRGO

Even though most persons think of Virgo as being an Earth sign making up more "grounded" persons, that is not always true in this case because your LDN is ruled by Mercury. Mercury and Uranus can create a lot of activity and motion. This could be a dynamic duo of natures, more likely to write books about their explorations and discoveries.

Sexually, you can be a dynamic duo of energies in the bed, sometimes taking an earthy, passionate approach and other times, a more dreamy and mystical one. Your lover/lovers can expect a diverse exchange in the bed. They will never be sure of what or how the lovemaking may go. Who wouldn't like to be surprised and delighted like that?!

LDN 7 / LIBRA

You are an extremely non-conforming free spirit, a true adventurer. Adventures, even those that are a bit dangerous, are your best "high". You love the adrenalin "rush" and some of you LDN 7 / Libra's can become addicted to following a life of high adventure. If you chose this type of life-style, you will have to expect moments of loneliness and isolation. You love your friends and family but you can't put a stop on your lifestyle to stay in one place with a job or routine that may bore you to death!

Sexually, you are a rare and exciting experience for your lover/s. If you can find someone who can keep up with you, that has the same addiction to adventure, you can be with them and remain faithful without a problem. For others that just pass in and out of your life, they will always remember the experience and be there for you if you should ever meet up with them again.

LDN 7 / SCORPIO

If you were a member of a tribe deep in the jungle, you would surely be the "Witch Doctor". Your "cosmic" sensitivities mixed with your innate knowledge of the secrets of nature put you above the average person. You are an interesting person and can be charming in company, but you mostly prefer to be on your own and free to explore life.

Sexually, you are intense and passionate in bed. Your lovers will easily fall in love with you because you are so fascinating and "hard to get" (for good), that is. Everybody wants something that is not easily acquired. When you fall in love, you become "captured" by your own obsession to keep that person locked into your "web".

LDN 7 / SAGITTARIUS

The lucky planet, Jupiter, rules Sagittarius. This LDN 7 is in for a lucky life. You will have high adventure, many interesting journeys and quite a few magical experiences. You are a charming, well -spoken person and would be a good public speaker. You could perhaps give lecture series at Universities about the discoveries you've made in your travels. A book would probably come firstly.

Sexually, you are a fiery, passionate lover, usually with a fairly high sex drive. You enjoy sex like you would a good meal. You're at ease in the bed and like to try cosmic techniques of lovemaking, like Tantric Sex for example.

LDN 7 / CAPRICORN

Yours is a conflict of natures. LDN 7's are free spirits and adventurers, but Capricorns don't have time for adventures. They are too busy climbing up the mountain to success. They are earthbound and immersed in their work. This conflict of energies may cause a slight tug of war within you.

Sexually, you have much the same problem as you do in your every day life because of your conflicting nature. One part of you wants to fly into the "Cosmos" with your lover while the other side wants to stay close to the earth, get it over with and go back to work. A few Capricorn males can be so attached to their mothers that they sometimes can't get over feeling ashamed of making love (because), Mother may not approve.

LDN 7 / AQUARIUS

You possess a perfect union of natures. Uranus with Uranus. The whole of you is in perfect harmony. With the illumination of conflicts, you are free to fly into the Cosmos you feel such an affinity with and party, party, party. You are a pretty "far out" person and have wonderful information to hand down to others for their enlightenment.

Sexually, none of this earthy "humping" for you. You prefer the more cosmic union. Certainly, you are a long time student of the many "higher" ways to create or increase the cosmic energy between you and your lover/s. Tantric Sex studies are a must for you.

LDN 7 / PISCES

With this pair of natures that match so perfectly, you would be successful and happy doing deep-sea studies and explorations. You are a gentle, sweet natured person and well liked by all. There is nothing offensive about your personality. You are not the most out-going person but can do well with one on one relationships.

Sexually, you are a sensuous lover and would probably be happier making love in a bathtub, pool or other body of water than in the bed, (unless it was a water bed!). Anywhere you choose, it will be a "heavenly" union. You enjoy sex to its fullest and make a good lover for the person that can respond to you on the same level. You select your lovers carefully because you're not promiscuous and you need each encounter to have meaning.

LDN 8 WITH SUN-SIGNS

LDN 8 / ARIES

Wow! Here are two Mars power signs blended together making up one nature! Eight is the number of power and prosperity. Aries, also ruled by Mars reinforces the LDN 8 and makes it doubly powerful. You are destined to rule some domain, whether it is a country or corporation, etc. Certainly your nature will urge you to take over and "organize" whenever you can. If you choose not to take charge of anything at all, you would be wasting your God-given abilities.

Sexually you are a powerful lover but don't always have the time to pay full attention to lovemaking unless you are intent upon "conquering" someone. Your sex urges are strong so you often seek release but don't always have time to devote to romancing, lengthy foreplay or courting. You are often on "overload" and too occupied with your various projects.

LDN 8 / TAURUS

Yours is a powerful combination of natures. Your Taurus sign ruled by Venus allows you to have some added qualities of romance in your nature. You are a multi-tasked person and could be some sort of artist or involved in the art world as a hobby or business. You are well liked but can tend to become a bit possessive of your close friends.

Sexually, you are an ardent lover and can be romantic as well. When you make time to devote yourself to love, you can make your lover/s very happy. You can be faithful if you're in love because you are generally too busy to be promiscuous.

LDN 8 / GEMINI

You use the power of your combined energies to develop your artistic career and push it in the right direction to gain success. You are very artistic, good looking and have a magnetic quality, so you could be a successful movie star.

Sexually, you are highly sexed and enjoy a variety of lovers. It is difficult for you to stay completely faithful to one person, even if you love them madly, but you try because you don't wish to mess up the direction and plans you have made for your career.

LDN 8 / CANCER

Your Sun-sign combined with the LDN 8 produces a person who can run a large corporation and pay attention to the needs of their family at the same time. Family and home are important to you so need to make sure the home-fires are kept burning for your return each day. You may try to control your family too much, so watch out for that.

Sexually, you are a caring lover. You try to put enough time aside to attend to your lovers' needs as much as for your own. You can be faithful if you have committed yourself to a relationship.

LDN 8 / LEO

Talk about taking Control, Bossiness and Power! You have it all! All these qualities can either work for you or against you depending on what career you have or are pursuing. Certainly, you cannot work FOR or UNDER anyone. You have to be the boss. You are very capable of being a leader of a country or director of a corporation. Just be careful not to take these leadership qualities home with you if you are a male. Your children and wife would not appreciate being bossed around all the time.

Sexually, you are a dynamic lover and enjoy delighting your lover/s with expensive, extravagant gifts. Since you are a multi-tasked person, you could be caught answering your phone during the sex act and to the amazement of your lover, never miss a beat!

LDN 8 / VIRGO

Your combined natures are a bit softer or a milder blend than the one above. You don't crave to rule your life and everybody in it like an Emperor. You are more concerned with getting the job done as best as you can and finding success in that. You are very ambitious and don't mind working hard to achieve your goals. You are a meticulous person, concerned with order, cleanliness and hygiene. Mercury which rules your Sun sign could sway you into a career as a journalist or something else in the field of communications.

Sexually, you are a good lover for someone who is not too adventurous in the bed. Your nature requires straight sex without too much intricate foreplay. As a LDN 8, you have a good, healthy sex drive. Your Sun sign, Virgo gives you an earthy, passionate nature.

LDN 8 / LIBRA

Your war-like, conquering nature combined with your Libra Sun-sign has a good chance of succeeding. Your combination of natures allows you to charm your way to the top along with your capabilities. People are attracted to you and like inviting you to their parties. You are attractive looking and your air of power adds to your appeal.

Sexually, you're a combination of power with romance thrown in to give your encounters a more interesting and inter-acting quality. You take the time to see that the "scene" is set with a romantic atmosphere. You don't forget the flowers, candles, music, etc.

LDN 8 / SCORPIO

You can be a dangerous foe with the combination of your power number 8 and your underworld planet, Pluto. People better take heed to be straight with you and not try to pull the wool over your eyes. They will be punished if they do. Ouch! your sting can be super powerful and destroy someone if you wish him or her to be destroyed.

Sexually, you can capture anyone you desire with little or no effort. Once you get them into the bed, they don't have much chance of escaping your desires and strong will, but then, few will want to because you can be a fabulous lover!

LDN 8 / SAGITTARIUS

You have few boundaries or limits as to how far you can go on the ladder to success. Your combine's natures of power and luck are on your side. You are fiery, exciting and very good at what you do. Your lucky planet, Jupiter provides all the luxuries and wealth you could desire. The trick to maintaining wealth is to be generous to the less fortunate.

Sexually, you are a joyful lover. You are sure to see that your lover/s have a good time and reach fulfillment. But, you can never promise them your very fullest attention. You are usually preoccupied with your many projects.

LDN 8 / CAPRICORN

You're one of the hardest working LDN 8's there are. You don't have time for much socializing. You prefer to work late into the night. That is your "pleasure". Getting to the top of the heap is of foremost importance for you and you don't mind climbing up for it.

Sexually, you can be a wonderful lover when you find the time to devote yourself to it because you sometimes get so immersed in your work that you forget about sex. If you are a male LDN 8/Capricorn, some of you wouldn't mind watching your lover/s performing with others in front of you. If you are female, you would make your sexual union with your full time lover as part of your "duties" as a good partner and respond to his needs even if you were not particularly "turned on" at that moment. This is not to say that this combined nature has little sex drive. You certainly do, but it depends on how much importance you give to it and how and where you direct it.

LDN 8 / AQUARIUS

Your combined natures can prompt you to pursue a career as a scientist, doctor, or biologist. Whichever you choose, you will become successfully noted in the journals of that particular field. You also could choose to head a conglomeration of Social or Charity organizations. You can do any of the above jobs very well because you have the natural intelligence, skills and compassion to accomplish it.

Sexually, you are a good lover if you feel in union with your lover in all the ways your nature demands. Friendship, spiritual and psychic connections are most important to you. That may be hard for you to find since you are so busy with your work, but who knows? Maybe the Gods will be kind to you.

LDN 8 / PISCES

You can be very successful because most LDN 8's are extremely ambitious and capable. Your field of interest and success could be the easiest if you consider your combined natures and head for watery careers like deep-sea explorations, etc. Remember, you are a powerful "fish".

Sexually, again you do your best near or in water. We can call you an "underwater sex expert"! But no kidding, your sexual urges, desires and excellence are best found near water. You are a good, strong and yet, "dreamy" kind of lover.

LDN 9 WITH SUN-SIGNS

LDN 9 / ARIES

With both planets Mars and Neptune guiding you, it is likely that you would have the type of career that would focus on helping humanity. The influence of your Warrior nature induced by the planet Mars and indicates that you would probably be a lawyer or politician of someone who would fight for the rights of the under-dogs and deprived of the world. No matter what you choose or chose to do, you would battle on like a mighty warrior and find success and satisfaction.

Sexually, you are a dynamic, sensuous and considerate lover. You are a nice blend of what your combined nature yields. Your lover/s should have no complaints.

LDN 9 / TAURUS

You are as earthy as you are spiritual. That can be an interesting blend. You acquire success through hard work. Part of your nature is bound to the earth and earthly things, whereas the other part of you is akin to the cosmic energies. Wouldn't be a surprise to anyone, if you decided to start up an organic vegetable or fruit farm. If you do that, you will find high success. You also may write a book on nutrition.

Sexually, you bring the best of both worlds to the sexual act and bring a lusty quality as well as a cosmic element to the bed. Your lovemaking is passionate and earthy with a degree of spirituality connected to it.

LDN 9 / GEMINI

Your combined nature, under the influence of the two planets Mercury and Neptune is a creative one. Your Gemini nature influences you to fluctuate from one thing to another. That is because you get bored easily. You like variety in your life. You're a good-looking person and can be quite charming when you want to. Your magnetic aura attracts.

Sexually, sex encounters come easily to you. Between your good looks and your magnetism, you have no trouble attracting lovers. You're not the most faithful lover because your nature requires variety. You enjoy having several lovers lined up, waiting for your call.

LDN 9 / CANCER

This is a watery combination so there could be some emotional ups and downs here. But that is not the main thing about you. You are a true and loyal friend and if a parent, a devoted one. The only problem you have is your overly sensitive nature that can cause you more grief than it does others. You are lucky to have the LDN 9 part of your nature to pull you out of your Cancerian bouts of doubt and depression. Sometimes you get panic attacks and try to cling on to the security closest at hand.

Sexually, you a faithful, thoughtful lover. Your approach is romantic with a little dash of cosmic energy thrown in. You are particularly aroused when making love in a tub, swimming pool or big body of water like a lake or the sea.

LDN 9 / LEO

No problems here. Your Leo, Fire sign dominates most of the time to help protect your more inward nature as a LDN 9. The Leo characteristic in your personality act as sort of a "cover" for you to disguise and sometimes promote your noble deeds and intensions. The fiery, dominating facet of your personality is what can launch a project and get it off the ground.

Sexually, your approach is cosmic, romantic and very passionate in a showy, glittery way. You like to lavish your lover/s with gifts and trips so long as they give you the adoration you like.

LDN 9 / VIRGO

Your combination of natures indicates a lovely cosmic, honest and almost "innocent" kind of person. Your motives are noble and you work hard doing your humanitarian or sociological work. You will work very hard to get tasks accomplished without wasting time because you are efficient.

Sexually, you are a good lover, more passionate then Cosmic although that aspect is not entirely ignored. Your lover/s has nothing to complain about. Your love is pure and you can easily remain faithful. You are not a "run-a-round".

LDN 9 / LIBRA

This combination of natures is Venus and Neptune, daughter and father of Mythological tales. Your LDN 9 influences makes you more serious minded, whereas, your Libra personality depicts a more romantic, playful, light-hearted person who adores enjoying all the pleasures life has to give. You are very good- looking and sexually attractive to the opposite sex so admirers are abundant. You are invited out to parties and such quite often.

Sexually, you can be a true delight. You are very romantic and also cosmic in your approach. You don't have problems having lovers waiting in a cue for your attention. You like deep, loving relationships but don't often stay for too long of a time with only one person. You don't like many lovers at the same time, but you are more likely to have a series of short, intense affairs, rather than one long one.

LDN 9 / SCORPIO

You are an "inward" mysterious person. It is rare when someone can unlock the door to your inner being. Outwardly, you are cordial and pleasant, but you don't allow people to get too close. You can do wonderful work for the poor and needy because that's what you enjoy doing.

Sexually, you can be a wonderful lover once you let someone in to your "private world'. After they are locked into your "Sanctuary" with you they will experience sensuous, cosmic, sexual delights they will never forget!

LDN 9 / SAGITTERIUS

Your ruling Jupiter planet brings you good luck both in love and money. You like to travel and usually can afford to do so. You enjoy darting around the world as a "World Traveler" and have friends in many different countries. Once you settle down to family life, you will make a good spouse and parent, but you will continue to crave the traveling even though it will be reduced to a more moderate scale

Sexually, you are passionate and exciting. You have a zest for life that is "catchy". You also have your cosmic side, which makes you even more fascinating. You attract, and then keep the attention of your lover/s. You're not one to get bored with easily.

LDN 9 / CAPRICORN

Your dual natures can sometimes draw you into a state of frustration. One side of you would like to believe that the energies of Universe guide you in all that you do. That isn't always possible because your Capricorn, Saturn planet urges you to do it yourself and climb to success no matter how difficult the journey to the top of the mountain may be. You have a good personality but there is always that secret place in you that very few can reach.

Sexually, you can be cosmic and very passionate but you are sometimes too preoccupied with your inner conflicts to participate with your whole heart all of the time. Your Capricorn nature includes being a bit of a "Voyeur". Your lover/s may suspect that when you make suggestions about your desire to see them making love with others. If they like that side of you and you are lucky, they may be prepared to provide "entertainment" to satisfy your whims.

LDN 9 / AQUARIUS

You are like a double LDN 9 or a double Aquarius because the characteristics of your Sun-sign and your LDN are virtually the same. Your theme song could be, "Come Fly with Me" because you are so connected to the cosmic energies of Universe. You would like to live in a better world, but you know that you can't change It so you try to do the best you can for yourself and others, to make life more bearable and joyful. You are a true humanitarian and probably find work as a social worker or a Psychologist to help people cope better with their lives.

Sexually, you don't set the world on fire with your passion, but you can display affection and love. You like to think of the sex act as a "union" of body, mind and spirit. That's what makes you the happiest.

LDN 9 / PISCES

Here we have another water combination that means you are not the most happy-go-lucky person in the world. You are more serious in thought and intent. Your nature is sweet and giving. Pleasing people you like is your greatest pleasure. You are well like because of these qualities.

Sexually, you are a tender, sensuous lover. You are gentle and more passive than aggressive and can be quite "self-less". It is important for you to trust your lover/s so you can give of yourself freely without fear of betraying yourself.

CHAPTER XII

LOVERS GUIDE & COMPATIBILITY CHART

Romantic Numerology is a quick and accurate way to match persons' natures. This guide will make it easier for the reader to select their more perfect mate to insure a more lasting and successful relationship.

GENERAL CHARACTERISTICS OF THE 9 LDN's AS LOVERS

<u>LDN 1</u> = Full of their ruling planet's (Sun) electric and Yang energy, you can bet on them being extremely ardent, passionate and somewhat aggressive lovers, although aren't known for their great romanticism. They like to get right down to it without wasting too much time on foreplay. Their nature is to take the lead, so their lovers never feel undesirable!!

<u>LDN 2</u> = Filled with the Yin energies of their ruling planet the Moon and their keen intuitive instincts direct them to knowing when you are in the mood for sex or not. They are sensitive lovers who know when, where, and how. Males are particularly good lovers as the Moon's feminine nature allows them to be "tuned into" feminine needs.

Foreplay plays an important role in their approach to lovemaking. You can depend on their loyalty if they are in love with you.

LDN 3 =The energies of their ruling planet (Jupiter) and the aura of their colour yellow, makes them very attractive. They ATTRACT and are natural FLIRTS so you can't be the jealous type with them. In the bed they can be very playful and create a mood of fun in their lovemaking. They are not moody or easily irritated so you can approach them with your desires at any time. Waking them up in the middle of the night to comply with your needs would find them receptive!

LDN 4 = Their ruling planet, (Saturn) can make them appear serious minded but don't you worry. There is a lot of passion lurking beneath their surface. When they make love, they do so ardently and totally with "all they've got"! You just have to be aware that they are very hard workers so they need to be relaxed and loosened up at the end of the day. They have a bit of the "voyeur" in them, so a sexy striptease could do the trick to stir up their sense of fantasy, which lies hidden behind their exterior. You can always depend on them to make an effort to make you happy.

LDN 5 = Ruled by the planet (Mercury), they are constantly moving both mentally and physically. They are very exciting and interesting persons but are sometimes misunderstood. They appear to be flighty because they are natural flirts. If you are lucky enough to have a LDN 5 lover once in your life, you will be lucky because you never will forget how much fun and excitement you had. They are sensuous, romantic and super interesting, even in the bed. They love to explore various ways and places to make love. You can be sure that a LDN 5 will never bore you. You may worry that they will not be true to you or stay with you for long, but if they fall deeply in love and you can live with their Mercurial nature, they will be completely faithful to you. The only thing that can't be guaranteed is if it will be forever. Their key word is "CHANGES".

LDN 6 = Ruled by the planet (Venus), they can't help but be extremely romantic lovers. Rose petals on top of the bed sheets (usually satin), a bottle of champagne by the bed, soft, sensuous music playing in the background, etc. should be no surprise. These things are all a display of their romantic nature. and come naturally to them. They are intent on "pleasuring" you to the oomph degree! In return, they need a lot of attention and affection. That shouldn't be so hard for you to give, considering what you are getting!!

LDN 7 = Their ruling planet, (Uranus) makes them fascinating. They are Cosmic with a scientific approach to it. Some can lean to mystical, occult interests. Don't be surprised if they ask you to join them in new, sometimes abstract techmiques of love-making. They have a keen imagination and are likely to want to spend some "dirty weekends" in different locations to add "spice & vinegar" to your sex life . They are the explorers, so be prepared to explore with them. Sometimes, they may seem to be "turned off" and aloof. Bear with this occasional quirk of their nature. They are only dreaming and "exploring" new thoughts and ideas in their mind.

LDN 8 = Their ruling planet (Mars) makes them lusty, fiery and powerful lovers. As the forever "conquers", they like to be in control most of the time. You don't have to worry about them being distracted by the other sex. They are multi-tasked persons so usually too busy with their various projects. But don't worry, when they turn their attention to "pleasure" you will be sure to receive the "Full Monty". Don't let their mobiles ringing in the middle of a sex session disturb you. It's par-for-the-course when you're involved with a busy LDN 8!

LDN 9 = Here you are dealing with an ancient Spirit, so expect to go to the heavens with them. Their ruling planet (Neptune) urges them to seek ways of taking the sexual union to a higher, cosmic plain. Friendship and understanding are the basis of their long-lasting sexual unions. They possess the ingredients that allow them to make your union a more "Cosmic" one. Don't be surprised if they introduce you to Tantric Sex!

<u>COMPATIBILITY CHART</u>

<u>LDN's</u>

1 + 1 = A dynamic duo but may be a bit too competitive and lock horns. "Hot, Hot, Hot"!

1 + 2 = Nice but 1 could lose patience with 2's intense sensitivity and emotions. So,so "Hot".

1 + 3 = Never a dull moment, great sex and social life. "Hot, Hot"!

1 + 4 = An excellent match if LDN 4's remember to let LDN 1 take the lead. "Hot"!

1 + 5 = Dynamic Passion, excitement and creative energy between them. 'Hot Hot"!

1 + 6 = Would get good loving but may not always appreciate 6's overly romantic approach to sex. "Hot"!

1 + 7 = May work if 1 has patience 7's mystical, free spirited thoughts. The sex can be good but not overly, "Hot"!.

1 + 8 = Dynamics, passionate sex and successful business partnership if 8 can let 1 be the boss. "Hot, Hot, Hot"!

1 + 9 = Harmonious and dynamic sex if you can accept your differences. "Hot"!

2 + 1 = Same as 1+2 above

2 + 2 = Very much alike so would be deep understanding between you and good mystical kind of sex life! "Hot"!

2 + 3 = May find them too happy-go-lucky and too playful in bed. "Hot"!

2 + 4 = Good stable and secure relationship. Harmonious in and out of the bed. "Hot"!

2 + 5 = Two very different people, would be intrigued by the sexual variety each could provide. "Hot"!

2 + 6 = Compatible and nurturing relationship. Romantic and emotional sex. "Hot"!

2 + 7 = Could fly to the moon together. Might have good sex for a While but may not last. "Hot"!

2 + 8 = May be too powerful, busy and controlling for you but could be dynamite sex. "Hot"!

2 + 9 = An understanding and interesting match. Their watery elements will bond them. Promises "far-out", (outer space)-like sex! "Hot"!

3 + 1 = Same as 1 + 3 above

3 + 2 = Same as 2 + 3 above

3 + 3 = A relationship charged with creativity and fun both in and out of the bed. "Hot, Hot"!

3 + 4 = Not the ideal match but could work in bed if 4 isn't tired too often. "Hot"!

3 +5 = An exciting, creative combo both in and out of the bed. "Hot, Hot"!

3 + 6 = A sweet, creative and loving combo. Sex is hot creative and romantic. "Hot"!

3 + 7 = A good match with much potential. Creative, fun, (with a drop of cosmic energy) in the sex. "Hot"!

3 + 8 = Dynamic sex but may not always have enough time to "play" with you in and out of the bed. You may feel neglected or get bored. "Hot, Hot"!

3 + 9 = Possible out of the bed, but VERY good in the bed if you are in love. "Hot"!

4 + 1 = Same as 1 + 4 above

4 + 2 = Same as 2 + 4 above

4 + 3 = Same as 3 + 4 above

4 + 4 = Could get a bit dull in time as you are both serious and hardworking. The sex is a lusty encounter, sometimes can be like a marathon! "Hot, Hot"!

4 + 5 = Too much contrast in natures. 5 would leave 4 feeling insecure about the relationship. But the sex can be great!!! "Hot, Hot"!

4 + 6 = Harmonious and fulfilling sexually. A lot of trust would be there between you. "Hot"!

4+ 7 = 7 may be too much of a dreamer for 4 but then again, it has possibilities of working. "Hot"!

4 + 8 = An excellent match of dynamics. It is a work concentrated

union. Hot & heavy sexual encounter! "Hot, Hot, Hot"!

4 + 9 = Could be a compatible relationship in and out of the bed if 4
can float with 9's cosmic energy. "Hot"!

5 + 1 = Same as 1 + 5 above

5 + 2 = Same as 2 + 5 above

5 + 3 = Same as 3 + 5 above

5 + 4 = Same as 4 + 5 above

5 + 5 = Very stimulating and exciting but not much stability, but if your
a 5, you don't care! "Hot, Hot, Hot"!

5 + 6 = 6 is too clingy and nurturing, would make a 5 feel stiffled.
Good sex in the beginning. "Hot, Hot"!

5 + 7 = Ideal. You can fly to the moon together and explore life and
all aspects of sex!! "Hot, Hot, Hot"!

5 + 8 = Dynamic and interesting sexual encounter. You will be
fascinated with each other. "Hot, Hot, Hot"!

5 + 9 = Is possible, but might prove a bit dull. Sex life could go either
way. "Hot"!

6 + 1 = Same as 1 + 6 above

6 + 2 = Same as 2 + 6 above

6 + 3 = Same as 3 + 6 above

6 + 4 = Same as 4 + 6 above

6 + 5 = Same as 5 + 6 above

6 + 6 = Ideal, could fulfil one another's' needs in love and sex. "Hot"!

6 + 7 = Has possibilities of working well both in and out of the bed.

"Hot"!

6 + 8 = Difficult because 8 can't give you the attention you need, nor enough romantic sex. "Hot"!

6 + 9 = Can be beautiful both in and out of the bed. Just don't give 9 the "rush" when you meet. They need time. "Hot"!

7 + 1 = Same as 1 + 7 above

7 + 2 = Same as 2 + 7 above

7 + 3 = Same as 3 + 7 above

7 + 4 = Same as 4 + 7 above

7 5 = Same as 5 + 7 above

7 + 6 = Same as 6 + 7 above

7 + 7 = Excellent match. You could "fly to the moon" together both in and out of the bed. "Hot, Hot"!

7 + 8 = Not very compatible. You are too "dreamy" for 8. "Hot"!

7 + 9 = Compatible in their mutual cosmic and spiritual interests. Will work very well in and out of the bed. "Hot, Hot, Hot"!

8 + 1 = Same as 1 + 8 above

8 + 2 = Same as 2 + 8 above

8 + 3 = Same as 3 + 8 above

8 + 4 = Same as 4 + 8 above

8 + 5 = Same as 5 + 8 above

8 + 6 = Same as 6 + 8 above

8 +7 = Same as 7 + 8 above

8 + 8 = Dynamic but competitive, lots of fighting but then lots of

"making up"!!! "Hot, Hot, Hot"!!

8 + 9 = Can be a deep love and harmony. Sex would be dynamic and spiritual at the same time.

9 + 1 = Same as 1 + 9 above

9 + 2 = Same as 2 + 9 above

9 + 3 = Same as 3 + 9 above

9 + 4 = Same as 4 + 9 above

9 + 5 = Same as 5 + 9 above

9 + 6 = Same as 6 + 9 above

9 + 7 = Same as 7 + 9 above

9 + 8 = Same as 8 + 9 above

9 + 9 = Can be a deep understanding and bond between you which can ignite "out of this world" sex. "Hot, Hot"!

SUCCESSFUL CELEBRITY COUPLE COMBINATIONS

FOR EACH OF THE LDN's

LDN 1 WITH LDN'S 3, 4, 5, 6
CELEBRITY COUPLE WITH ONE OF THE ABOVE COMBINATIONS:
Mathew Vaughn (1) & Claudia Schiffer (5)

LDN 2 WITH LDN'S 4, 6, 7, 9
CELEBRITY COUPLE WITH ONE OF THE ABOVE COMBINATIONS:
Prince Charles (2) & Camilla Parker Bowels (9),

LDN 3 WITH LDN'S 5, 6, 7, 8

Richard (3) & Judy (7)

LDN 4 WITH LDN'S 1, 2, 6, 8
CELEBRITY COUPLE WITH ONE OF THE ABOVE COMBINATIONS:
Kevin Federline (4) & Brittney Spears (6)

LDN 5 WITH LDN'S 3, 5, 7, 8
CELEBRITY COUPLE WITH ONE OF THE ABOVE COMBINATIONS:
Catherine Zetta Jones (5) & Michael Douglas (7)

LDN 6 WITH LDN'S 2, 4, 6, 9
CELEBRITY COUPLE WITH ONE OF THE ABOVE COMBINATIONS:
Victoria (6) & David (2) Beckham

LDN 7 WITH LDN'S 2, 3, 5, 9
CELEBRITY COUPLE WITH ONE OF THE ABOVE COMBINATIONS:
Guy Richie (7) & Madonna (2)

LDN 8 WITH LDN'S 2, 4, 5, 6
CELEBRITY COUPLE WITH ONE OF THE ABOVE COMBINATIONS:
Oliver Martinez (8) & Kylie Minogue (9)

LDN 9 WITH LDN'S 2, 5, 6, 7
CELEBRITY COUPLE WITH ONE OF THE ABOVE COMBINATIONS:
Kursten Dunst (9) & Paul Bettany (5)

PART II

CHAPTER XIII

PROFILES OF CELEBRITY COUPLES

CHAPTER XIV

PROFILES OF CELEBRITY INDIVIDUALS

CHAPTER XIII

PROFILES OF CELEBRITY COUPLES

TONY BLAIR   LDN 2 (MOON/WATER)
CHERIE BLAIR   LDN 6 (VENUS/AIR)

Both of their ruling planets are both feminine, (Yin) in nature. This makes theirs, an ideal match. Their union is one bonded in harmony. They have a natural support system between them because their LDN'S (Life/Destiny Numbers) as well as that their Sun-signs compliment one another. They have an un-dying loyalty between them. UNITED THEY STAND". A large part of this bonding is created in their bed. Tony is earthy, intuitive, sensitive and emotional making him a perfect "lover for Cherie. She compliments his nature with her combined Sun-sign Libra and LDN 6 because they are both ruled by Venus. This makes her extremely feminine, sexy, loving, loyal and nurturing. She needs a lot of attention but Tony's awareness of this keeps him on his toes. This LDN MATCH is perfect and should be enduring.

GEORGE BUSH LDN 6 (VENUS / AIR)
LAURA BUSH   LDN 8 (MARS / FIRE)

Our little Laura's powerful LDN 8 nature reveals that she is the real, not "power", but rather "strength" behind the throne even though she comes across as the sweet, "southern bell". The true "power" behind the presidential seat comes from other supremely powerful, dominating sources. George is like a "misplaced person" in the role of the worlds' MOST POWERFUL LEADER. His LDN 6 nature is not an ideal one for the making of a World Leader. He undoubtedly would never have been able to accept this "role", had it not been for Laura's promise of her sworn support. Her powerful LDN 8 nature and organizational skills enables her to be his "back-bone". Laura and George make a good couple. He offers affection and love, while she offers the loving support he needs. All in all, they are compatible and will endure as a couple because they each need the other to make a "whole". This LDN MATCH is a good one and will endure.

BILL CLINTON   LDN 2 (MOON / WATER)
HILLARY CLINTON   LDN 3 (JUPITER / AIR)

Bill, as an LDN 2 is extremely magnetic therefore very attractive to women. If he got all the love and affection he needed at home, this man would never have strayed. LDN 2's are generally loyal and sensitive. It is not their natural way to cheat on their partner/s, neither in love nor business. Hillary as a LDN 3 is the one who normally should have the flirtatious nature. She was born with the natural skills to charm and delight everybody when/if she wants to. Somehow, somewhere along the line, these two stopped "holding hands" and their relationship lost its way. So many things have passed between them and so much trust has been lost, it is doubtful that they will ever be able to even catch a glimpse of the love sparks that first brought them together. The only thing they have together at this point is to maintain whatever loyalty that remains in their relationship as friends and try to do their polite duty to one another for the good of both of their political careers and their daughter. This LDN MATCH has burned down to mere embers with no hope of sparking into flames again.

SHARON OSBOURNE   LDN 1 (SUN / FIRE)
OZZIE OSBOURNE   LDN 1 (SUN / FIRE)

Although appearing to be the "ODD COUPLE", they are relatively well matched.   SHARON, as we all know, seems to "Rule The Roost", but if Ozzie were not so dissipated and dependent on her as he appears to be, he would be more the "Leader of The Pack" than she. They are both LDN 1's which makes this match a constant contest of wills. Sharon's more stable and balanced nature allows her to rule the roost better.   Ozzie's two fire life forces create great clashes of dynamic energies within him. That and his musician's life-style has obviously burned a lot out of him out at this point of his life. There is a strong bond of loyalty and love between them but it is doubtful if there is a lot of "hot" sex going on in their marital bed these days, (but then, you never know!!) Her devotion to him and his need of her, besides the love they share, is what holds this couple together. They have their occasional battles when both want to be the "Leader Of The Pack", but Sharon's Libra, Venus sense of balance and harmony guides her as to how "handle" him. This match has been challenging, to say the least, but seems to have worked out well. Somehow, this LDN MATCH works. It certainly began as dynamic and fiery and now seems to have mellowed.

MADONNA   LDN 2 (MOON/WATER)
GUY RICHIE   LDN 7 (URANUS/FIRE)

Madonna was born with the most opposing combination of Sun Signs and LDN's That exist. These create a constant battle /pull within her. The feminine, sensitive energies of her LDN 2 nature constantly struggles to rise above the masculine, dynamic energies coming from her fiery Leo Sun-sign. One minute, she is a very feminine, vulnerable woman and the next a commanding, bossy "She-Man". Guy as a LDN 7 has a mystical, free-spirited side to him which matches well with Madonna's LDN 2 intuitive nature. She excites him and keeps him busy (and sometimes frustrated) trying to figure her out and keep up with her contrasting natures and the frequent changes they put them both through. He excites her with his good looks, probing mind and spiritual, "seeking" qualities and fills her with a feeling of security because he is such a solid, grounded, family man. Their sex-life is

133

diverse. They both have the mixture of earthy, dynamic, mystical, cosmic and sensitive sides to their natures. Their sexual union surely is never dull when it happens. It can sometimes be very dynamic with Madonna playing her dual roles. Sometimes she is the masculine aggressor and at other times, passive, romantic and feminine. Guy can sometimes disappoint her when he goes into one of his "inner sanctuary" modes and doesn't want to be bothered by anyone or anything. Much of their sexual relationship depends on whether their contrasting natures come together in balance at the same time. When their natures are in opposition, it can be disappointing for them both. You might say that their sex-life is like the "roll of the dice". This LDN MATCH can endure if both of them make an effort.

CHRIS EVANS   LDN 2 (MOON/WATER)
BILLY PIPER   LDN 6 (VENUS/AIR)

Their LDN's 2 & 6 are both feminine (passive) in nature so their sex life is harmonious, romantic and sensitive. Whatever problems they may have, they can always "make up" in the bed. Chris response to her feminine and giving nature and becomes a considerate, ardent lover. His LDN 2 makes him exceptionally sensitive to Billy's sensual and sexual needs. His timing is most often perfect! Billy is an extremely loving and nurturing woman, but she has to be careful not to make Chris feel smothered by her constant need to make him feel loved.   The opposite natures of their sun-signs could be the cause of the recent problems they have been having, but the compatibility of their LDN'S will always keep them attracted to each other. This LDN MATCH is ideal.

KERRY McFADDEN   LDN 6 (VENUS/AIR)
BRIAN McFADDEN   LDN 7 (URANUS/AIR)

Their LDN's, 6 & 7, although not the most ideal number combination, can work well together. They are both Air signs which make them compatible.   Kerry is a creative, sexy, romantic Venus woman determined to surround herself with beauty. Brian is a dynamic, dreamy lover, but at time can be withdrawn and preoccupied by his wanderlust to discover the mysteries of life.   This could be misinterpreted by Kerry as a sign of disinterest in her.   Brian's withdrawals could create a gulf between them but Brian will fight to keep them together. This LDN MATCH can work, (but, sometimes like a seesaw).

RICHARD MADELEY   LDN 3 (JUPITER/AIR)
JUDY FINNIGAN   LDN 7 (URANUS/AIR)

They are both alike and at the same time different enough in natures to hold one anothers' interest. Richard's LDN 3 makes him forever youthful in both looks and thought. LDN 3's inherit the skill of allowing the "young child" within them to stay free and alive throughout their lives. He is creative, magnetic, good looking, playful and a bit of an "adventurer". Although Judy is a bit older than he, she is kept young in spirit and mind by his influence. Her LDN 7 nature is a curious one with a fascination and need to probe into things of curiosity and mystery. She is a free spirit, always seeking higher knowledge which keeps Richard fascinated. Their sex life is varied. Sometimes it can be fun and playful. At other times can have a touch of the "cosmic" and/or "spiritual". I wouldn't be surprised if they haven't contemplated trying "Tantric Sex techniques"! This LDN MATCH is a very good and enduring one because they compliment and have invested a lot in each other.

CLAUDIA SCHIFFER   LDN 5 (MERCURY/AIR)
MATTHEW VAUGHN   LDN 1 (SUN/FIRE)

Claudia's LDN 5 with its influence of Mercury gives her the need for constant changes for her growth and development as a person. She is forever changing. Matthew's LDN 1 nature is dynamic and masculine in its' electric energy. He is equipped to keep her "in line" when she goes too far outside of it. She keeps him fascinated with her multi-facetted nature and interests, but he definitely takes the lead (most of the time) in the bed and their domestic life. This LDN MATCH is not a perfect one by numbers, but can happily endure if the love between them is strong. He is her strength. She is his delight.

PRINCE CHARLES   LDN 2 (MOON/WATER)
CAMILLA PARKER BOWELS   LDN 9 (NEPTUNE/WATER)

It is no wonder that Camilla was able to control Charle's emotions for so many years.   Her LDN 9 reflects a "knowing" which makes her easily understand his nature and needs. She has the wisdom to know what his "buttons" are and how to use them to keep him devoted to her. With the intuition of a LDN 2, he has an affinity to the feminine nature and needs and this makes him super sensitivity, (almost delicate in nature) and extremely emotional. Their sex life is probably full of fantasy-and role playing. That and their intimate "secrets" could be the core of their relationship. This match may "run the course", but only for public view.   Now that she has accomplished her goal to marry Charles, she will find it more difficult to hide her true colours. She may not continue to "enchant" him as she did when she was his "secret". This LDN MATCH can work if Charles doesn't get bored with it now that much of the "fun" of their relationship is gone having become a publicly known "legal union" and no longer a "secret thing".

QUEEN ELIZABETH   LDN 7 (URANUS / AIR)
PRINCE PHILLIP   LDN 2 (MOON / WATER)

Here, curiously enough, we have the very same match of LDN's 7 and 2 as Prince Charles and Princess Diana. Things between Elizabeth and Phillip turned out differently because this couple had a different, more conservative up-bringing in another generation. Those facts combined with Elizabeth's position as Queen of Britain surely had a big influence on their marriage maintaining its respectability with no hint of scandel. Phillip's LDN 2 nature makes him a very sensitive, emotional person. His Moon influence makes him particularly "intuitive" and matches Elizabeth's "awareness" and sense of curiosity about mystical, "unknown" things. Surely their sexual union must have had a few "cosmic moments" when they were young. Elizabeth is a curious LDN 7 who is constantly seeking her own inner truth as well as the truths of life. She is interested in all people, their ways and customs and what makes them "tick". This makes her a very interesting person to be around. Just take care not to bore her! She is not interested in being in the company of persons' who don't have anything interesting to say or that can not inform her of curious things she hasn't yet learned. This LDN MATCH is a compatible one by numbers and will continue to endure amicably.

DAVID BECKHAM   LDN 2 (MOON / WATER)
VICTORIA BECKHAM   LDN 6 (VENUS / AIR)

Their LDN's are perfectly matched. He having the LDN 2 makes him a sensitive person and lover to match her needs. As a woman with the LDN 6, ruled by Venus, she gives and needs enormous doses of affection and attention.   Sexually, they are well matched but their daily life is not so easy. She finds it difficult and refuses to take a "back seat" to his fame and charisma. She also has had a hard time dealing with his LDN 2 magnetism that attracts women to him like bees to honey. She wants him all for herself and you can't blame her. This will be a constant and continuing struggle for Victoria with her sensitive nature and inflated ego. David, on the other hand has to contend with Victoria's overwhelming love which can sometimes be felt as "smothering" and too "mothering".   This LDN MATCH has a good chance of surviving because it is a perfect match of numbers,

CATHERINE ZETTA JONES   LDN 5 (MERCURY/AIR)
MICHAEL DOUGLAS   LDN 7 (URANUS/AIR)

A perfectly matched couple. (almost fairy-tale like) their same Sun-signs balance one another. both are air signs so they fly side by side. Her LDN 5, the number of changes keeps him fascinated. His LDN 7 the number of the "seeker", a curious nature interested in the occult and mysteries of life is right up her street. In bed, I would guess that they often fly up to merge with the energies of Universe (probably with a stop over on the planet, Venus. All in all, they make a pretty perfectly matched couple. This LDN MATCH is perfect and has a long course to run.

BRITNEY SPEARS   LDN 6 (VENUS/AIR)
KEVIN FEDERLINE   LDN 4 (SATURN/EARTH)

This match of LDN'S should/could have been a perfect one if Kevin had proved to be a true LDN 4. Britney's LDN 6 nature makes her extremely romantic and feminine with a deep need to love and nurture in such a way that sometimes could be interpreted as "smothering". He, on the other hand turned out to be untrue to his LDN 4 by being demanding, thoughtless, head strong and self centred. His LDN 4 (should have) lead him to taking the relationship seriously and to giving her the stability, sense of security and support she needed. Their sex life was "hot" at first until he became too pre-occupied structuring his own ambitions. This must have caused Britney to worry and be scared that he was no longer interested in her, (except for what she could do for him).   If she had been smart enough to keep him as her live-in lover instead of legal husband, she could have maintained more control over the relationship. But, as a LDN 6, she followed true to her need to seek that "perfect love" and give all of herself. She allowed the ball to fall into his court while he had a "sexual spell" on her. Now, she has finally come out of that "spell" and sees him for what he is. Good for her to begin action to get him off her back. His only "cat in the bag" is their babies. Watch out

Britney, he will not give up easily and try to bleed you dry counting on

your loving Number 6 nature. This LDN MATCH could have been a

perfect one (by numbers) if Kevin had been true to his LDN 4 nature.

DEMI MOORE   LDN 4 (SATURN/EARTH)
ASHTON KUTCHNER LDN 7 (URANUS/AIR)

Couldn't call them a perfectly matched couple according to their

above LDN's, but Demi could be attracted to his LDN 7 which leads

him to curiosity for the mystical, cosmic and occult. Her LDN 4 makes

her the "Big Mama" so perhaps Ashton is just the son she never had.

Her LDN 4 keeps her grounded and a hard worker who needs to build

up her own financial and family security. Her nature needs to

structure and build her life upon a firm foundation. Ashton gives the

impression of being more concerned with his own future at the

moment although he "claims" that his primary interest lies in his role as

a father and husband. He is more independent in nature than Demi

although he needs and values her advice and guidance in his new

showbiz career.   In bed they can soar into the upper levels of the

Cosmic world, but not every time.   Their sex life is intense if not

passionate. She may think that she has more chance of keeping him

in tow now that she has introduced him into the sacraments of the

mystical Kabbalah, but I wouldn't count on that, Demi. You also

introduced him to the glittery Hollywood film world. How is that going?
This **LDN MATCH** is not especially ideal, (as an LDN combo) and with
their age differences, but seems to work in this case.

WILL SMITH   LDN 4 (SATURN/EARTH)
JADA PINKETT SMITH   LDN 4 (SATURN/EARTH)

Will and Jada don't have much to argue about. They are both LDN
4 so their fundamental motives and needs are similar in that they both
put great importance to hard work and their family life. Their children
and their own relationship come before their careers or social life.
Will, being a Libra is the more creative and airy one who enjoys
pursuing a few fantasies now and again. He puts the magic into their
lives. Jada as an Aries is the fiery one, perhaps more the leader. Both
are devoted to each other and are devoted parents. Their love life is
varied. If it begins to get a little humdrum, you can be sure that it is
Will who livens it up (in his romantic Libra way) and whisks Jada off for
a romantic and sexy weekend. Jada can be exciting and the more
aggressive one a lot of the times. This **LDN MATCH** looks pretty
perfect!

CALLISTA FLOCKHART   LDN 6 (VENUS/AIR)
HARRISON FORD   LDN 8 (MARS/FIRE)

They have a double plus on their relationship because of a natural
and most INTENSE attraction to one another created by their Sun signs.

Their LDN's also indicate compatibility. Callista having the LDN 6 is a romantic, demanding and nurturing lover. Surely Harrison has learned by now that he better never show a wondering eye in her presence. She would FLIP. He on the other hand, is not really the type to wander very far from home. His LDN 8 makes him a powerful and ardent lover when he's not too preoccupied with his many projects. His maturity guide him to giving Callista the attention and nurturing she needs to keep her happy. She will always be responsive to his desires. This LDN MATCH is a very good one.

HUGH GRANT   LDN 7 (URANUS/AIR)
JEMIMA KHAN   LDN 7 (URANIUS/AIR)

Hugh and Jemima are a natural couple. Even though their sun signs may sometimes conflict, their mutual LDN 7 keep them in tune with each other. Both are free spirits but Hugh is a little more grounded than Jemima because of his earth sign Virgo. He likes everything to be in order. She is easier about perfectly kept drawers, etc. They both have a need to seek higher knowledge and awareness. In bed they fly to the moon. It wouldn't be a surprise to learn that they will eventually pursue higher levels of pleasure and take a Tantric Sex course (with me, of course) to make their union more complete on a spiritual level. They have a good chance for their relationship to grow and be lasting if Hugh can learn to kerb his need for perfection and lose his "cold feet" for commitment. This LDN MATCH has excellent possibilities.

JESSE WALLACE   LDN 7 (URANUS/AIR)
DAVE MORGAN   LDN 6 (VENUS/AIR)

Jesse is a romantic being who lives for the most part for LOVE. She can withdraw though into her inner thoughts and leave Dave feeling a bit left out sometimes. He has to understand that she, as a LDN 7 she is a constant SEEKER. She has a curiosity for the unknown and must be given the freedom to continue her search throughout her life. His LDN 6 Venus nature makes for an ardent, romantic lover. In bed they enjoy an exciting, romantic and sometimes very intense love – making. For sure it is always emotional and loving on his part. She has to learn that Dave needs a lot of nurturing and affection to keep him happy. This LDN MATCH is not a perfect one, but if the love stays strong, is possible.

NIICHOLAS CAGE   LDN 1 (SUN/FIRE)
ALICE KIM   LDN 7 (URANUS/AIR)

Alice may be the perfect woman for Nick! She is a young, sweet LDN 7 who is up for adventure. Being oriental, she has learned to serve and obey her man. Nick is a bossy LDN 1 so he can't stand a woman who stands up to him. He needs to be the boss, nothing but the boss. He wants to have his cake and eat it too. When he doesn't want to know that she is around, he leaves the house or shuts himself up like a recluse and nobody better disturb him. Sexually, Nick can be an ardent lover but not always the most thoughtful one. That is not a problem because Alice is happy to comply with his demands although she would like to explore the various aspects of sex, if he is agreeable. She will never be demanding of him. I expect that she will adjust to his ways and moods and will bend to his ways to please him. Her LDN 7 is a good match with his number 1. She enjoys time to herself to dream, study and explore things with her mind. This LDN MATCH though not absolutely perfect, has a good possibility of surviving.

KATIE HOLMES   LDN 1 (SUN/FIRE)
TOM CRUISE   LDN 1 (SUN/FIRE)

Ho! Ho! Ho! Mr. Cruise is in for a big surprise! His role as "Napoleon" in their relationship is going to be short lived. Katie with the same LDN as his is already rearing her Number 1 head to give him a "run for his money"! Tom is much older and has garnered more fame, status and money than Katie but her two combined fiery natures will assure that she will soon catch up with him. She may even get sick of taking orders from him altogether and just pack up and leave one day. He will fight to the end to keep his family together or at least, to keep their daughter, should they break up. Unfortunately for Katie, he has more money, thus POWER, to get his way. Good thing her father is a clever lawyer. But, clever enough to fight Hollywood Big Wigs? Surely she is "betwixed and between". There aren't too many ways out for her at this very moment and she may not want to get out of it really, because they do have happy moments together when he puts on his charming and caring ways that lie behind his "Svengali" mask. Their sex life is guaranteed to always be exciting and dynamic. This match could be the greatest if Katie were older, more experienced and more famous so not to fall "victim" to Tom's manipulations. If Tom could learn what love really is and love someone more than he loves himself, they would have a better chance. As it stands, it doesn't look like this relationship will not have a "Happy Ending" in the long run though it will be a super fiery relationship as long as it lasts! This LDN MATCH is packed full of dynamite and fire with flickering flames that can go out at any time!

GOLDIE HAWN   LDN 6 (VENUS/AIR)
KURT RUSSELL   LDN 9 (NEPTUNE/WATER)

Goldie's LDN 6 nature helps to keep Kurt from sinking too far into the watery Piscean depths of dispair when those moments come to him. It also keeps him feeling secure that he is loved. Most of the time he is content to let her nurture and love him as a number 6 can. He is supposed to be the more spiritual one with his LDN 9 influences, yet Goldie is the one who seems to seek more Cosmic experiences than he does with all her trips to India, etc. But, who knows? He was born as the "Wise Old Spirit", so perhaps he has a built-in spirituality that he doesn't make an outward show of. Whatever experiences they may have together, both good and bad, their sex life and basic spiritual connection will always hold them together. This LDN MATCH is pretty perfect.

NANCY REAGAN   LDN 8 (MARS/FIRE)
RONALD REAGAN   LDN 2 (MOON/WATER)

Allow me to explain the secret ingredients of this couple's success and rise to power together! Nancy, having the LDN 8 was the real POWER behind Ronald's throne. She was born with the ability to organize and the power to run such a huge conglomerate of corporations such as a country like the USA. Ronald had the compassion, loyalty and intuition to be the "Face", believe in Nancy and go along with her plans and encouragement. His LDN 2 nature gave him the power to envision things on a higher, futuristic plain. Nancy was devoted but must have disturbed him sometimes, when she made him feel less like the free spirit he wanted to be and held him tightly in the control of her number 8 powers. This LDN MATCH worked because LDN2 is magnetic energy and LDN 8 is electric. (Yin and Yang)

MELANIE GRIFFITH   LDN 3 (JUPITER/AIR)
ANTONIO BANDERAS   LDN 7 (URANUS/AIR)

This is a windy, passionate union. Two Air signs under the same roof make for an exciting, glamorous atmosphere and the possibility of clashes when they battle for who is the most interesting and exciting. Antonio, having the LDN 7 is more matured in his outlook and behaviour. Melanie's LDN 3 makes her more "airy fairy" (like the eternal child she is). They are both creative, but she is more than he. They share a lot of interests together and their sex life is dynamic, generous, passionate and playful. LDN's 3 & 7 are most often very good together. This LDN MATCH is an excellent one.

JULIA ROBERTS   LDN 7 (URANUS / AIR)
DANNY MODER   LDN 3 (JUPITER / AIR)

Here is another combined match of LDN's 3 with 7. This LDN combination seems to be an enduring one but not without its many ups and downs. Danny as a LDN 3 is the "lighter" of the two. He brings a playful aspect into the relationship which works on the more serious minded, intense nature of Julia. Danny's nature makes him eager to live a fun, easy-going life. He is creative and lucky so he doesn't worry about doing well. His only problem is dealing with Julia. She is often filled with doubts and can become pessimistic in her thinking. With the LDN 7, she is always SEEKING and digging for the essence of everything. That part of her fascinates Danny. Julia took her time seeking the perfect match for herself and now that she has made her choice, she is determined to make it work. If she is in hopes that the children will make their marriage ever-lasting, she may be right. The relationship works because Danny manages to get her out of her sullen moods and thoughts with his light-hearted attitude. He creates "fun" in their lives. Of course, the basic ingredient of any match is LOVE. If that is there, it is possible to find happiness. The LDN MATCH is an excellent one.

LIZ HURLEY   LDN 1 (SUN / FIRE)
ARUN NAYER   LDN 3 (JUPITER / AIR)

Arun has his hands full with this dynamite LDN 1 lady, ruled by the Sun! She was born with incredible energy-force. He must enjoy having a dominate lady in his life because that's what he has. In and out of the bed, things will usually go as Liz wants them to. He, on the other hand is a playful, creative, lucky, attractive LDN 3 who will never lose his child-like approach to life. He will always stay young in spirit and bring fun and games into their lives. Liz was wise in choosing a younger man and even luckier, a LDN 3. He will submit to her bossy nature and bring fun into her life. She just has to be careful not to be too dominating and learn to make her demands in a softer tone. Maybe, she has already learned how to do this because they have been together for a few years now and are planning to marry. Here's wishing them good luck! This LDN MATCH is not ideal but also is not impossible if the main ingredients to any relationship; love, respect and humour are there.

JENNIFER ANNISTON   LDN 2 (MOON / WATER)
VINCE VAUGHN   LDN 3 (JUPITER / AIR)

Well, if this sensitive, emotional "Moon Lady" couldn't make it with a man like Brad Pitt who was the ideal LDN 4 match for her, she may or may not have better luck with the not so perfect LDN 3 match with Vince. Perhaps Vince has learned the art of "lightening" Jennifer up. He obviously must have learned how to "walk on eggs" by now as well as how to give in easily to her wishes. She is lucky to have found a lively, playful guy who has a sensitive streak in him as well. It could be that her relationship with Vince will bring out the better side of her nature because he is more accommodating to her demands than Brad was. But, let's see how long Vince will continue to bow down to her self-centred demands. It is doubtful that he will be able to persuade her to give in to his wishes and dreams sometimes instead of only her own, but he can try. She is a very ambitious, determined person who may never find her ideal, perfect man because (she is not as perfect as she thinks she is) and only thinks about her own dreams and goals. It is almost sure that she isn't going to commit to any relationship until she is absolutely sure that there is no way of getting Brad back, (and that may be, never). This LDN MATCH is not one to make any bets on. It doesn't have much chance of surviving as a "Winner".

ANT McPARTLIN   LDN 6 (VENUS / AIR)
LISA ARMSTRONG LDN 9 (NEPTUNE / WATER)

This is one of those ideal matches. Ant is a loving, nurturing being. He gives and needs a lot of affection. He is creative and has wonderful taste. He knows how to "set the scene" for gracious dining, love making, etc. Lisa, as a LDN 9 is the wise old spirit with a great understanding of most things. She is a compassionate and loving humanitarian. Their relationship doesn't have many "bumps" in it. Once they marry, they will easily maintain the compatible relationship they have established over the years. This LDN MATCH is excellent.

SANDRA BULOCK   LDN 8 (MARS / FIRE)
JESSE JAMES   LDN 5 (MERCURY / AIR)

This LDN match of 5 and 8 seems to be a popular one according to the matches found in this book. They excite one another and keep each other going. Sandra has to take care though, not to become too controlling, (the bad trait of a number 8). Your number 5 guy won't take too much control. LDN 5's are probably the most unlikely to be controlled! They are the freest of the free spirits! But, she must have found this out by this time, so as long as she respects and accepts his Mercurial changes, they will be alright together. She finds his non-conforming ways interesting and exciting. He loves her dynamic warrior-like nature and her multi-tasked mind. This LDN MATCH is a lively and excellent one as long as the love lasts.

BARBARA STEISAND   LDN 9 (NEPTUNE / WATER)
JAMES BOLIN   LDN 3 (JUPITER / AIR

Barbara is the compassionate LDN 9, the "wise old spirit". She is also known for being a perfectionist and getting a little "heavy" about things sometimes.   James is the perfect ingredient to ease her sometimes tortured soul and miserable, perfectionist nature.   He can be envisioned as a lovely piece of yellow crystal that brightens up her spirit. He is an extremely attractive man who any woman would enjoy having as her own. She, on the other hand makes him see things in a more practical and serious light. With the wisdom and understanding of her LDN 9, she guides him as a Master would guide a Disciple. He with his light hearted LDN 3 nature is able to influence her to be more flexible and easy-going.   They are both creative beings, so can dream up projects to do together. They seem to have mutual respect for one another and their separate careers, so that is good. This LDN MATCH is a good one.

MARTHA STEWART   LDN 8 (MARS / FIRE)
CHARLES SIMONYI   LDN 8 (MARS / FIRE)

Whoppa!! There are a lot of sparks in this relationship. Both having the LDN 8 makes for an extremely dynamite union. They will lock horns often but it will never get dull. Both are strong willed and controlling so we have to wait and see which one (if either) becomes the conqueror. Both of them are rich and successful so there is no competition there but if they are wise, they will never attempt to work together. They have a good chance of having a wonderful, dynamic relationship if they stick to their own jobs. As number 8's, they will both be so busy with their own projects that they will probably have to make appointments to see each other! That's how number 8's are; very distracted by their work. If they learn to make the best of their intimate time together and not step on one another's toes, they can be very happy. This LDN MATCH is a dynamic and interesting one.

CELINE DION   LDN 3 (JUPITER / AIR)
RENE ANGELIL   LDN 6 (VENUS / AIR)

How's this for an enduring, ever-lasting match! Their LDN'S are good together because Rene gives Celine her creative freedom and oodles of love and affection. LDN 6's have extremley loving and nurturing natures. Celine is much younger than Rene and he has had her under his wing since she was a mere girl but she must like the situation and certainly has garnered high success through his management of her career. It is a father / daughter and husband / wife combination that seems to be bonding them for life and that's not a bad thing. She must be a more serious minded LDN 3 who has learned not to give too much vent to her free-spirited nature. She puts all that into her career and that's not bad either. This LDN MATCH is a happy one and will endure.

HEIDI KLUM   LDN 9 (NEPTUNE / WATER)
SEAL   LDN 8 (MARS / FIRE)

This couple doesn't have many problems getting along. Seal is a dynamic, ambitious LDN 8 nature with a passion to succeed. He is also a multi-tasked person so can easily deal with several projects at the same time. Heidi is a beautiful woman but she no doubt has learned to wait patiently for Seal's full attention. Number 8's are always so preoccupied with their projects / work that they find it difficult to just "turn off" to relax and enjoy the company of their loved ones as much as they should. Seal would never dream of turning off his phone while making love so it could go off during a sexual encounter, interrupting the whole thing. He is lucky that Heidi is a lovely number 9 with patience and understanding. She is the "wise old spirit" so she is able to persuade him to change his ways a bit at a time so they can enjoy their lives without too much interruption. She enjoys his passion and respects his ambition but has to be careful not to put out his fire. This LDN match has possibilities.

ELTON JOHN   LDN 4 (SATURN / EARTH)
DAVID FURNISH   LDN 3 (JUPITER / AIR)

David's LDN 3's light and cheery nature keeps Elton from getting too serious and overworking himself. Elton's LDN 4 nature can lead him to being a "workaholic" so he is lucky to have David's influence to slow him down so he can enjoy life to the fullest. David is a perfect match for Elton. Their union is all about give and take. Elton with his stable and sensible, loyal LDN 4 nature gives David a sense of security and stability. David may be a bit of a flirt sometimes but it is usually innocent, just part of his playful nature. Elton shouldn't let it bother him. This LDN MATCH is an excellent one with possibilities of a long run.

DENISE RICHARDS   LDN 1 (SUN / FIRE)
RICHIE SAMBORA   LDN 6 (VENUS / AIR)

This couple is best according to their ruling elements Air and Fire more than their LDN's. Denise as a LDN 1 is a bit too dynamic and bossy for a more easy-going LDN 6, like Richie. Maybe she helped him through his break-up of his marriage, but this relationship is not ideally matched for a long term relationship. Sure, right now they are madly in love because they both needed one another after their break ups with their spouses but there can be bets taken as to how long it will last. They are not mismatched and have a fair chance but it never is too good when the woman is the dynamic and bossy LDN 1. The sun energy that rules her gives out a very dynamic and masculine energy. This LDN MATCH could or could not endure. We have to just wait and see, but don't bet on it.

KYLIE MINOGUE   LDN 3 (JUPITER / AIR)
OLIVER MARTINEZ   LDN 8 (MARS / FIRE)

This is a lively combination. Kylie's happy-go-lucky energy surely lightens up Oliver's more intense, ambitious nature. He may try to control her at times but will soon learn that this would not go over too well with her and her free nature. She is creative and he is the "organizer". Actually, if they've learned to share their natures, they could do very well together in helping one another with their careers. This LDN MATCH is a good, workable one.

COURTNEY COX   LDN 5 (MERCURY / AIR)
DAVID ARQUETTE   LDN 8 (MARS / FIRE)

This couple obviously is well matched because it seems that before everything else, they are best friends. LDN's 5 and 8 make an exciting combination of natures. They are both lively, exciting and ambitious.

It looks like their enduring relationship has formed a kind of "nation of two" together. They have many friends but don't seem to allow them to influence their own relationship no matter how confused they may be sometimes. This LDN MATCH is excellent and seems to be enduring.

SARAH JESSICA PARKER   LDN 4 (SATURN / EARTH)
MATTHEW BRODERICK   LDN 4 (SATURN / EARTH)

Well, what a solid match we have here!! They are both hard working, loyal and work together to build security for themselves and their children. They are both solid as rocks! If and when they have spats or differences of opinions, they work hard to come to an amiable compromise. They WORK at working out everything. They are devoted to one another and are excellent parents. My guess is that when they feel it's the right time, they will have more children. As LDN 4's they hold their family life above all else. This LDN MATCH is excellent and enduring.

UMA THURMAN LDN 5 (MERCURY / AIR)
ETHAN HAWKE   LDN 7 (URANUS / AIR)

This LDN match is ideal. LDN's 5 and 7 are terrific together! She keeps Ethan interested and excited while he takes an avid interest in everything she does or says. He finds her fascinating because she is like liquid Mercury, always moving and changing. He loves this. LDN

7's just can't stand boring people. They are so interesting themselves; they need to be in stimulating company. Uma is ideal for the role of being Ethan's "main lady". This LDN MATCH is terrific and should endure.

SIEGFRIED FISCHBACHER   LDN 6 (VENUS / AIR)
ROY HORN   LDN 4 (SATURN / EARTH)

LDN's 4 & 6 go well together. Together they form a loving, secure union. Roy as an LDN 4 is the hard worker and more likely to being the more ambitious of the two. Siegfried as an LDN 6 is a hard worker as well, but more on the creative level, like creating the sets for their act and decorating their home and he strives for harmony in the relationship. He is more interested in loving and nurturing the animals and Roy than only making money and achieving success. They recently had a big set-back which throws their whole lives off track and I'm sure drove a nail between their relationship but they have to remember that everything happens for a reason. Maybe the accident was meant as a message to slow down and perhaps change their lives around a bit? This LDN MATCH is a good, solid one.

GWYNETH PALTROW   LDN 2 (MOON / WATER)
CHRISS CROSS MARTIN   LDN 2 (MOON / WATER)

What a watery, "Moony" couple we have here! I wouldn't be surprised if they occasionally wake to find that they have shared the same dream the night before. They must be closely bonded because LDN 2's can be extremely intuitive and mystical. Their sense of loyalty to one another is strong. They don't have to sing the song, "Fly Me To The Moon". They are already there together! They are bonded by their deep communication with each other. This LDN MATCH is a strong union. (I wonder if their next child will be named "Strawberry" or "Plum?!")

ORLANDO BLOOM   LDN 2 (MOON / WATER)
KATE BOSWETH   LDN 6 (VENUS / AIR)

Here we have another compatible LDN match. Orlando has himself a Venus woman to delight and stimulate him with her creative energy and romantic nature. Kate is loving and nurturing in nature besides possessing the beauty and attractiveness of a Venus woman. Orlando is a sensitive LDN 2 who may sometimes sink into a sulk or two if or when he feels that he has been offended. Kate wouldn't have too much patience with this behavior but her good nature will try to get him out of his emotional doldrums. It isn't always possible, but she will always make an effort.   Male LDN 2's are senstitive lovers and attractive to women, so Kate may just be content to "hang in there" until they make love again. This LDN MATCH is an excellent one and has possibilities of enduring.

BRAD PITT   LDN 4 (SATURN / EARTH)

ANGELINA JOLIE   LDN 5 (MERCURY / AIR)

Poor Brad! That may sound like a strange thing to say about a man who was lucky enough to get a gorgeous woman like Angelina but I have to say that because their natures contrast so much. Brad as an LDN 4 is solid as a rock. He will never leave Angelina and the children but the same can't be said of Angelina. If anyone leaves the other it will be Angelina making the break.   Brad has a steady, steadfast nature and his devotion to his family will always come before his career. Angelina, on the other hand is a wonderful human being and mother but her LDN 5, MERCURY vibration urges her to make constant changes. She will never be happy living in one place for too long whereas Brad can stay in one home in one place for his entire life. He is an earthy, solid man made to be a loyal husband and terrific, caring father. It is not only difficult for him to keep up with Angelina's Mercurial nature, it is painful! No doubt there is a passionate and true love between these two but the extreme contrast of their natures may create an increased wedge between them as time goes on. This LDN MATCH, as beautiful as it looks, doesn't have much chance of surviving happily ever after.

NICOLE KIDMAN   LDN 4 (SATURN / EARTH)
KEITH URBAN   LDN 5 (MERCURY / AIR)

Poor Nicole! Yep, I have to say it again. She and Keith have the same difficult contrast in natures as the couple above. Nicole is an earthy, grounded LDN 4. All she wants is to be a good mother and wife. She can promise fidelity, loyalty and security. Keith, on the other hand is another LDN 5 with an airy, non conformist nature that survives and grows with continual CHANGES. No matter how much they love one another, it is going to be a constant problem for them to blend their natures into a harmonious brew for happiness. It will be most difficult for Nicole. Her LDN nature yearns for a solid, secure home life. Keith will always be on the road and tempted by drugs. He makes for an exciting husband and friend but hard to keep track of and down on the earth. She is "roots", he is "wings" (although her airy Sun-sign takes her up there with him a lot of the time). He gets the better of the deal though because Nicole will always be there for him, keeping the home-fires burning. This LDN MATCH is difficult but their love and need for one another can keep it going if Nicole understands and forgives him for being a LDN 5.

JUSTIN TIMBERLAKE   LDN 6 (VENUS / AIR)
CAMERON DIEZ   LDN 3 (JUPITER / AIR)

Both, being free spirited Air signs, Justin and Cameron's LDN match is a compatible one. Justin with his LDN 6 is the more loving and nurturing of the two even though he is younger than she. Cameron is more child-like. Her creative nature makes their union joyous and fun. LDN 3's never like to grow up. Her charm is her ability to allow her inner child to live freely and close to the surface. LDN 3's emit a joyous energy that attracts everyone. Justin is more romantic in his approach to sex. He likes to make a "ceremony" out of their lovemaking. She enjoys his romantic, caring approach and adds a little humor to it. This LDN MATCH is a compatible one, full of love and joy.

PAUL McCARTNEY LDN 4 (SATURN / EARTH)
HEATHER MILLS   LDN 1 (SUN / FIRE)

This relationship didn't have much of a chance for harmony from the start. It may have endured for a longer time though, if Heather had been able to know Paul's nature better. His LDN 4 indicates that he is a devoted family man and family comes before all. He also is a bit stubborn and stuck in his ways now at his age. Heather, on the other hand, is a dynamic, bossy LDN 1. Her fiery nature simply heated Paul up and scorched his (earth) energy and patience. Had they (read THE LOVE LOTTO) to learn of one another's natures', their relationship may have had possibilities of enduring for a longer time. She would have known better than to try to attempt to change his ideas and way of life. It may have worked if Paul was younger and not so experienced. But as it is, there is no hope of reconciliation. This LDN MATCH became a disastrous MIS-MATCH!

KATE HUDSON   LDN 4 / EARTH
CHRIS ROBINSON   LDN 9 / WATER
OWEN WILSON   LDN 8 / FIRE

This trio is an interesting study. Kate as a Number 4 is an ambitious, hard working, earthy and a devoted mother. Normally, Chris, being a Number 9, the "wise old spirit" with a natural understanding of nearly everything and a great deal of compassion would normally be an ok match for Kate. But, as in this case, the life styles of couples can often conflict and create friction. Owen, who seems to be Kate's choice of a more compatible match for herself is a dynamic Number 8. His fiery energy excites and inspires her much more than Chris's watery energy ever could. LDN 4's and 8's always make an excellent match. They both are extremely ambitious, organized and hard working. They can go far together by working together. They can create production companies and other businesses and in general create a productive, exciting life together.

CHAPTER XIV

PROFILES OF CELBRITY INDIVIDUALS

ANNA NICOLE SMITH
SAGITTERIUS (FIRE) LDN 8 (FIRE)

ANNA is a "ball of fire" and a "Warrior". Not surprising that she fought for years for her part of her wealthy husband's estate. She is not the type to give up easily. Her LDN 8 lends to her needing to control. She can do many things at one time with no difficulty. Although she may slip sometimes and give the appearance of being a bit of an "airhead" and out of control, but don't be fooled. She is a "survivor" and has a very strong Will to control those around her as well as her own life. She has many interests and a natural instinct for what is going on around her. Sex is not her main objective and never will be. It is a means to an end for her but she doesn't have a fierce drive for it. She enjoys her sex image and displaying herself as a sex goddess, but it is more of a "gimmick" she uses to garner fame and fortune rather to attract men.

ELTON JOHN
ARIES (FIRE) LDN 4 (EARTH)

Elton is motivated by his fire Sun-sign to forge ahead with his projects with no mind for the hard work may be involved. Hard work "turns him on" and makes him feel alive. His fire sign gives him the dynamic energy he needs and his LDN 4 gives him the will to work and create a firm foundation for his life to build upon. The LDN 4 depicts the mythological figure Saturn who was always busy forging steel repairing the other God's chariots. He often became so absorbed in his work that he would lose track of time and be content to sacrifice his own love life at times. I think that Elton went through that in his younger years. As he matured, he realized that he needed the intimate love of another person to make his life complete. If he didn't have a partner to divert him from his work a little, he could easily become a serious "workaholic". He is an excellent manager of his own life. He is a loyal and dependable friend, almost a Father figure that people can rely on for sensible, good advice. The eccentric side of his personality comes from the influence of his fiery Sun-sign Aries more than from his LDN 4, which is the more grounding, serious, and family oriented side of his nature.

SARAH JESSICA PARKER
ARIES (FIRE), LDN 4 (EARTH)

Sarah is head strong, a hard worker who needs to build her life upon a firm foundation into a solid, secure structure. Is no wonder that she has a successful career and marriage. She devotes equal time to both but if had to make the choice, would chose her family life over her career. She is a devoted mother and wife; grounded and reliable in nature.

Note: is no wonder that she locks horns with Kim Cattrall. Their natures are in direct contrast & conflict to one another's which can be noted in Kim's horoscope below.

KIM CATTRALL
LEO (FIRE) LDN 5 (AIR)

As a Leo, Kim is a born, "leader of the pack" a pioneer with courage. If she is in a situation where she is told what to do, she feels ill because she cannot take orders, though is good at giving them. She has got to be the boss. Her number 5 nature is one that thrives from making constant changes in her life. Her sexual nature is similar to that of the role she portrays in "Sex In The City". She soon becomes bored with her lovers in real life also, which makes her flirty and promiscuous.

NAOMI CAMPBELL
GEMINI (AIR), LDN 8 (FIRE)

Naomi gets her volatile nature from the energies of Mars that rules her LDN 8 and marks her as a Warrior. When their balance is tipped, a LDN 8 can be very controlling and prone to violent attacks (as this one is) upon those who oppose them. Her Sun-sign influences her to be changeable. It also marks her as a creative beauty. She gets bored easily. She can be very demanding and exciting in bed. She should find a Libra, LDN 4.

ROBBIE WILLIAMS
AQUARIUS (AIR), LDN 9 (WATER)

This guy is cool and calculating in both business and love. He doesn't appear to have any of the qualities of the "Wise Old Spirit" that a LDN 9 person normally has. His LDN 9 combined with his Sun-sign Aquarius is like a fusion of the same exact traits of wisdom, compassion and a caring humanitarian, etc. But, Robbie hasn't shown any of these qualities. His life and life-style is exactly opposite to what his Sun-sign and LDN indicates. He appears to be extremely selfish and self-centred without going out of his way to help anyone or anything. Story tells it that his father taught him all he knows about performing and initiated him into show business but now that Robbie is rich and successful, they say that he has made no effort or gesture to repay his father. I am suspicious of people like him who have no lips. They usually prove to be stingy. I suspect that he may be as stingy in bed as he is out of it. He could possibly take a lover to "cloud nine" once or twice to impress, and then get "hum-drum", routine and eventually disinterested when he feels any demand to give more. Guess we could say that Robbie is just not the most generous of persons and is certainly not true to the signs of his birth. Maybe time will change him??

COURTNEY LOVE
CANCER (WATER), LDN 9 (WATER)

This girl doesn't have much of a chance for happiness. She is as "watery" as one can be and doomed to have constant emotional ups and downs. She sometimes nearly drowns in the mystery, intuition, moods, and depressions that whirl around and encase her. Being so super sensitive, she often sees herself as a victim. Obviously drugs helped her to reach a level of un-consciousness to allow her to cope with all the dark corners of her mind. She just doesn't love herself enough and is self-destructive. Her energy attracts destructive forces which she can not control. It's a good guess that she likes a bit of "rough" in bed in her appeal for punishment. Anyway, she has a kind nature and does manage to be entertaining (at times). Does she remind you a little of Judy Garland?

HALLE BERRY
LEO (FIRE), LDN 8 (FIRE)

Halle is a very powerful lady contrary to the way the media portrays her. Her Leo Sun-sign makes her a Born Leader. She likes to have things her own way. Her LDN 8 controlling nature reinforces her dynamic and bossy Leo characteristics. The number 8 reflects power.

She also has an incredible brain that allows her to organize and perform multiple tasks. She can do several things at the same time without getting ruffled. It is hard for her to find a suitable life partner. She detests weak men yet will fight to try to over-power a strong man. She is feminine and very passionate but is surely aggressive, assertive and controlling in bed much of the time. I predict she will mount and run a successful production company of her own in the near future. She will have more success with that than with her love life.

PRINCE WILLIAM
GEMINI (AIR), LDN 2 (WATER)

Listen up girls; I can inform you that William with the LDN 2 is a good and sensitive lover! The influence of his airy Sun-sign makes him creative and diverse in bed as well; never boring. In general, he is a sensitive person, sometimes too sensitive and easily hurt. He gets along with his father most of the time because they are both LDN 2's and have similar natures, approaches and feelings about things although their Sun-signs make them very different. William's Sun-sign Gemini makes him a creative, magnetic, fun-maker. This creative part of his nature may lead him to taking up the hobby of painting or sculpting.

PRINCE HARRY
VIRGO (EARTH), LDN 1 (FIRE)

Harry has a strong and dynamic nature, is ambitious and very sure of himself. It's natural and easy for him to pursue projects on his own, as he sees fit. Consent or permission from his family will never deter him from doing exactly what he wants to do. He is a born leader, is ambitious and has his feet firmly planted on the ground. He is a passionate lover and will want a girl to share his passions both in bed and in projects, but she daren't not have too strong of a character to conflict with his or try to tell him what to do. He can be stubborn and will always want to take control and be the leader.

LENNY KRAVITZ
GEMINI (AIR), LDN 6 (AIR)

Lenny is a loving, nurturing man. He is creative and has good taste in music, art, wines and food. He likes a "voluptuous" life-style. He's not very lucky in love because he usually finds that he gives more than he gets. Because of his Gemini nature, he may appear too changeable for some women, appearing too unreliable and leaving them feeling uncertain about his true feelings or sense of commitment.

NICOLE KIDMAN
GEMINI (AIR), LDN 4 (EARTH)

She could have been the perfect LDN match with Lenny Kravitz but perhaps their same Sun-signs of Gemini clashed with one another. Nicole is a gorgeous, talented woman and a devoted mother. Her family life means most to her. As she has matured she seems to have grown more into a LDN 4 mode leaving her Gemini nature in a back seat. As a LDN 4, she seeks stability and to build her life upon a firm foundation. She can be a "work-alcoholic" and needs to be with someone who can draw out her Airy, changeable, fun-loving Gemini nature and encourage her to relax and have more fun. A LDN 3, 4, 6 or 9 would be her best matches but let's see how she does with her choice of a LDN 5 (also ruled by Mercury like her Sun-sign)!!

TOM CRUISE
CANCER (WATER), LDN 1 (FIRE)

Tom is basically a "home-body" with an incredible drive to of an LDN 1 to run the whole show.   His dynamic energy drives him to be the "Leader'. His Cancer nature loves having a family and is devoted to them but his Number 1 nature leads him to rule them with too much of an "iron fist". He has a natural drive to succeed and has been so successful that it seems as though he has conjured up a self image of a God-like figure in his own mind. He loves producing his own films because he needs to have "control"and be the boss. He must have the first and last word as a LDN 1. His Cancer nature makes him super sensitive and hard to forgive anyone who hurts him deeply. (not a hard thing to do). Seems like Tom has gone a bit "off the rails" and become a "control freak" with big Crab Claws!

DELTA GOODREM
SCORPIO (WATER), LDN 6 (AIR)

Not strange that Brian turned to such a woman for understanding when he broke up with Kerry. Delta's Scorpio nature is constantly probing into mysterious things and creates an air of mystery and sensuality about her. Her LDN 6 projects feminine, romantic and sensuous qualities (but with a little more sex and intrigue thrown in.) All in all, she is a sensuous, sexy, loving, loyal woman. What more could anyone ask for?

JENNIFER ELLISON
TAURUS (EARTH), LDN 9 (WATER)

Jennifer is an earthy girl, a bit possessive of her lovers and feels compassion for humanity. She is wise beyond her years and can go to higher levels of consciousness at times, but for the most part is down to earth in her approach, particularly her career. She plods along with ambition and plans. She is a good manager of herself and has a good idea of what her goals are. She goes towards them in a systematic way. In love, she gets her man, then holds tight reins on him and will not stand for any cheating. She is a passionate lover and will stay loyal until the end.

ANGELINA JOLIE
GEMINI (AIR) LDN 5 (AIR)

Angelina must live with constant movement and changes. Her LDN 5 is the number of CHANGES. Mercury ruling her LDN 5 also rules her Sun-sign Gemini which makes it doubly hard for her to stay in one place. She is unique and different from the average person because she is a non-conformist. The way she thinks and lives her life may confuse most persons because her ways are contrary to the rule. She grows with each change she makes in her life. Many may mistakenly interpret her constant changes as the mark of an unstable person because her behaviour and choices frighten them. But Angelina is a brave, free and courageous spirit. She lives her life as a "Spiritual Warrior" who leaps into the dark abysses with blind faith. It is normal for a LDN 5 to change lovers many times. She also could possibly make a complete change of careers at a later time in her life and leave acting behind one day to mark as "yet another experience". Keep an eye on her because she will surprise us all over and over again!

MADONNA
LEO (FIRE) LDN 2 (WATER)

Madonna's combined natures are a complete contrast to each other. Her Leo energy is masculine in nature while her LDN 2 ruled by the Moon is feminine. She has the constant pull of the Yin and Yang within her. On one hand, this can be the secret of her success as a performer while on the other hand, can be the reason why her personal relationships are so difficult. One moment she can be dominating, wanting everything to be one way, (her way or not at all). In that role, she is "electric", exciting and demanding. Then, she can suddenly switch to the role of a simpering, contrite and passive female. It must keep her husband and others close to her in utter confusion of whether to love her or hate her. But whichever of her two energies dominate her in a moment, she certainly is an interesting and exciting person to be around (if you don't mind getting a bit dizzy). This contrast of natures can be torture for her. It must be exhausting to cope and understand and keep in time with the two sides of her nature and personality. When her Leo Fire takes hold, she, as the "Lion", can growl ferociously and demand her way. Then in the next moment, reduce that "growl" to a soft purr of a contrite "pussy cat".

SADIE FROST
GEMINI (AIR) LDN 3 (AIR)

Sadie's choice of career as a designer is a perfect one for a creative LDN 3. LDN 3's are creative, magnetic and lucky so whatever she creates will always draw attention and success. She will always maintain her young spirit and want to "play". Her secret is the ability to keep the young person inside of herself forever alive. The influence of Mercury from her Sun Sign influences her to constantly make changes in her life, career, men, location, etc., It will be hard for family and friends to keep track of where she is and what she is doing because her changes will be sudden without much discussion with others. She will be motivated by her inner de-cisions. There aren't too many mistakes she can make because with her creative talents, she will always manage to not only survive, but to succeed. All her changes will lead to her growth as a person and artist.

LEONARDO DECAPRIO
SCORPIO (WATER) LDN 7 (WATER)

LDN 7's are like sponges soaking up life's energies. Leonardo will always be an extremist plunging into the life experiences that confront him. He is eager to explore everything life has to offer. He has the need to travel and have exotic experiences. Sexually, he is at the stage of exploring his own prowess. Scorpio's are very sexually intense. Leonardo is still quite obsessed with it, but can you blame him when women are throwing themselves at his feet because of his fame and fortune. He certainly doesn't ooze sex appeal. His body and poise are that of a young, inexperienced boy. I suspect that he is more awkward than "smooth" in the bed.

DAVID BOWE
CAPRICORN (EARTH) LDN 3 (AIR)

As an LDN 7, David was born blessed with creative talent, a magnetic presence and luck to succeed. His public may find it strange that he disappears and reappears again without giving notice. This is caused by the influence of his sun sign. Capricorns tend to retreat into a dark lonely space within their own psyches, sometimes for no apparent reason. David sometimes becomes an "untouchable" even to the persons closest to him. Luckily as an LDN 7, he can keep snapping back into positive inter-action so he can continue being a star for as long as he will allow himself to be. Sexually, he follows the same pattern. At times he will show great interest and intense sexual prowess in love making. Then, as suddenly as the mood comes upon him, it can leave and he can lose interest in everything and everyone.

CINDY CRAWFORD
PISCES (WATER) LDN 8 (FIRE)

We needn't wonder how Cindy rose to such exceptional fame and success. The power of her LDN 8 creates a very "together" lady who knows exactly what she wants and fights to get it. Her Pisces Sun-sign works on her inner self and emotions, the weaker part of her and can occasionally pull her off her "high-horse" to plumet her into a dark pool of depression. Luckily, her LDN 8 gives her the power to snap out of her gloomier moments quickly. Sexually, she has a healthy appetite and can be ardent and demanding. It's not a good idea to get in her way when she is devoted and concentrating on a project. She could be prone to shows of temper when annoyed or crossed.

GOLDIE HAWN
SCORPIO (WATER) LDN 6 (AIR)

Goldie has had one of Hollywood's' most stable relationships for many years. Her LDN 6 ruled by Venus enables her to maintain a balance and harmony in her domestic life but when or if this balance becomes impossible to maintain, it will be all over. It is well known that Scorpios' have enormous sex drives. This combined with her romantic Venus qualities makes it a good guess that a large part of her relationships both past and present were/are based primarily on sex. She will never let her life be turned upside down. She will seek balance and go forward with faith towards her destiny.

ASHLEY JUDD
ARIES (FIRE) LDN 2 (WATER)

Ashley, has a similar conflicting combination of fire and water as Madonna. Her sign, Aries is what drives her on to conquer all her difficulties and surge forward. It is her LDN 2 that pulls her down into emotional despair with doubts and pain. It is simply the conflict between the dominant male and female energies she was born under. One moment she has high and positive energy to be positive, know exactly what she wants and goes for it. On the other hand, when her Moon influences approach, she can sink into modes of doubt and weakness. The battle throughout her life will be to get over the Moon influences that partially rule her. But no matter how low she sinks, her Fire sign will pull her up to once again surge toward success.

JENNIFER LOPEZ
LEO (FIRE) LDN 3 (AIR)

J-Lo usually gets what she wants because she is very commanding and bossy as a Leo. Her LDN 3 nature is where her talent and good luck comes from. It also creates a magnetic aura about her, which is exactly what she needs to keep film, and music audiences en-raptured of her. This is a girl with a lot of luck. She just can't go wrong except maybe in her love life because she is not the easiest lady for a man, with his own large career, to get along with.

MARTHA STEWART
LEO (FIRE) LDN 8 (FIRE)

Fire with Fire are the ingredients which make up this successful woman. She is extremely independent and needs no one's help. Being a number 8, she has an amazing capacity to organize things and held big combines. It is no surprise that she has built herself up to being an Icon. If she had chosen politics, she would be giving Hillary Clinton a run for her money in the next election and my guess it that she would come out the winner. It would be easy as pie for Martha to be the President of a country like the USA but this may not taste so good to all as the real apple pies she bakes.

DUSTIN HOFFMAN
LEO (FIRE) LDN 9 (WATER

Dustin is dynamic and a leader but he also has a spiritual side. His LDN 9 depicts the "Wise Old Spirit". He possesses inner wisdom as well as compassion for humanity. . You can be sure he is active in many charities, although does not "advertise" those private activities. He is a kind man with a good sense of humour but can become quite egocentric, demanding and bossy at times. The nature of his number 9 helps to keep his personality more in balance.

GWYNETH PALTROW
LIBRA (AIR) LDN 2 (WATER)

Gwyneth's light and airy Libra Sun-sign creates a good balance with her LDN 2. The number 2 part of her gives her the characteristics of being very sensitive. It also makes her a loyal friend. Her Libra side gives her beauty and a creative flair. Put all this together and you can see how she became successful in the film industry. But also as a Libra, she may change her career and do something else creative like painting or designing clothes. Whatever she does, she will find gratification and success.

BRUCE SPRINGSTEEN
LIBRA (AIR) LDN 1 (FIRE)

This is a bit of a contrasting combination but one that seems to work for Bruce. Librans' are charming, romantic, easy-going, creative people more interested in love and romance than anything else. The LDN 1, ruled by the Sun is a dynamic, "go-getter". They are direct, can be calculating and are have to take the lead. That seems to explain how Bruce charmed his way to success as the "leader of the band", appropriately nicknamed, "THE BOSS".

CATHERINE DENEUVE
LIBRA (AIR) LDN 5 (AIR)

Catherine is still the beauty she was at the height of her career as a young woman. That is because she is a "Venus" woman. Libra women never lose their grace or beauty. LDN 5's stay young because they are always changing and making changes in their lives. Every time she makes a change in her life, she grows, but, not old. She will always maintain the aura of a beautiful, charming woman. (NEVER, an "old" woman).

ARNOLD SCHWARZENEGGER
LEO (FIRE) LDN 4 (EARTH)

The Leo part of Arnold is both the actor and politician. He is flamboyant and vibrates the energy of a Leader. His LDN 4 qualities of being a hard worker and creating the aura of stability are what make him successful at the things he wants to do. He is not afraid of hard work and has the patience to bide his time until the right moment comes for him to put his plans in motion. He loves being a high official because this allows the bossy Leo part of him to be the boss and give orders.

DREW BARRYMORE
PISCES (WATER) LDN 1 (FIRE)

Drew is a perfect example of this combination of energies. As we all follow her life, we see how she has conquered her demons with the strength her LDN 1 gives her. The Pisces side of her nature is what causes her problems. Pisces persons have tendencies to get lost in the watery depths of their emotions. This causes them more agony than they deserve. Most Piscean persons are very sweet and a bit vulnerable in nature. These qualities are what makes her such a sensitive actress and cause her fans to love her so much.

GEORGE CLOONEY
TAURUS (EARTH) LDN 1 (FIRE)

George can be quite a "hard cookie". He is demanding, commanding, bossy, aggressive, and stubborn as a mule although he has a compassionate, loving side which makes him a good friend to have. As a Taurus, he is ambitious and willing to work as hard as he has to in order to reach success. He is very good with business and money matters. His LDN 1 urges him to take the lead, not take any ones advice and only rely on his own convictions. He has got to have his own way! This may be why he hasn't found his big love yet. He is too occupied ruling his own life. Perhaps he should stay away from Hollywood actresses and find a simple woman who is not In show business to share his life with.

MONICA LEWINSKY
LEO (FIRE) LDN 5 (AIR)

Well no wonder!! Leo's go after what they want and LDN 5's are the "adventurers". Monica is an attractive, bubbly young woman who could attract many men. But she seems to have retreated quite a bit since the White House scandal. Staying in the USA in the shadows of her infamy isn't the wisest thing for her to do. She never gave herself the chance to let people see her in her own light. She should get out there like the LDN 5 she is and see the world, to have many more adventures and experiences while she sheds her "infamy". Then she can come back and start all over again as "Just, Monica", or (maybe even change her name)!

MICHAEL JACKSON
VIRGO (EARTH) LDN 6 (AIR)

Earth with Air and Mercury with Venus may give us a hint of what Michael is about. Basically, he has the emotional maturity of a 13 yr.

old boy. He is full of love and needs to display his affections but his Virgo earth side makes him feel shy, "naughty" and awkward doing that around adults. He feels safer and more secure when he is in the company of kids at the same level of maturity as himself. His Virgo side urges him to work very hard to achieve success, whereas his number 6 nature distracts his attention from work and drives him to seek and give the love he craves. He is a creative, kind soul struggling with his passion/obsession for LOVE but, he must change directions and take care to stay away from the intimate company of young children to stay out of trouble!

PARIS HILTON
AQUARIUS (AIR) LDN 2 (WATER)

Paris has gone way off base from the quality of her dual natures by pursuing the controversial career she has created for herself. But, then, there is always an exception to the rule. Aquarians are supposed to be wise and compassionate. The LDN 2 is very influenced by the Moon and is normally sensitive, intuitive, kind and loyal. Perhaps, the influence of her Moon somehow "zapped" the emotional, sensitive side of her nature during a full moon and turned her in the wrong direction? In the right state of mind and surely when she gets older, she will look back at all the wild things she is doing now and may cringe at the image she created for herself. It's going to be hard for her to change paths when and if she ever wakes up and realizes how she distorted the image of the kind of person she really is or could be. I predict she began her image making as a big joke to see if she could get away with it. If that is the case, when/if the time comes when she may want to change it, will find it will be too late to turn the public's impression of her around.

MICK JAGGER
LEO (FIRE) LDN 5 (AIR)

A Fire and Air combined nature makes for a whirlwind of energy. Sounds like Mick to me! He enjoys being the Lead singer in the group because he can't work with people if they are in the position to tell him what to do. As a Leo, he has to think of himself as the "Leader Of The Pack". (At least, the leader of himself). He has the drive and dynamic energy of a Leo combined with the independent, non-conforming nature of his LDN 5. Apparently, this combination worked for him. His LDN 5 nature is that of CHANGES. That explains why he has to change partners as often as he can. He just never can be a one-woman man, no matter how much he may try because he eventually gets bored.

RICHARD GERE
VIRGO (EARTH) LDN 8 (FIRE)

Richard's LDN 8 nature gifts him with the ability to organize. He is the organizer. He is also a multi-tasked person. It is apparent that he has always lived a very "organized" life. We never heard gossip about him that put him in a bad light. He never got involved with drugs and he is consistent in his work as a fine actor who never seems to go out of style. He gracefully eased his way from a sexy young man to a sexy "older" man. His boyish charm, which comes from his Virgo nature, will never be lost. Richard is here to stay. He has the number 8, the number of power and the Warrior. A Warrior such as he will never fall prey to the politics of Hollywood.

PRINCESS DIANA
CANCER (WATER) LDN 7 (AIR)

LDN 7 has the nature of the "Seeker". They are always seeking their own inner truth and the truth of life. They are spiritual and often the "Healer". Cancers are ruled by the Moon so they are very intuitive, sensitive and devoted to their families. Diana was a combination of the "SEEKER" and the "Home Body". We all loved her for the many good deeds she did for the poor and needy, respected her for being the devoted mother she was and excused her for being such a "mixed up girl". She tried her best to live by the two natures that guided her. Why it went all wrong for her so soon, we will never know? May you rest in peace, Darling Girl.

MEL GIBSON
CAPRICORN (EARTH) LDN 7 (AIR)

Mel's Capricorn nature is that of a "worker". It also contains a "secret chamber of darkness" within the psyche. The "worker" part of his nature may play a large part in making him the successful actor and director. His LDN 7 nature is more complex and leads him to need to explore his own and life's secrets. His combined natures makes him a difficult person to understand or get too close to, because both parts hold moments of inner isolation that can't be explained. Both his Sun sign and LDN hold natures that go inward quite often. Obviously, his recent problems are a result of prejudices that were ingrained in him as a young boy. But as a Capricorn, LDN 7, he automatically held the nasty thoughts deep within (like a secret). He grew out of them by using his own judgement as a grown man, but obviously there are still fragments left embedded in his psyche. He probably isn't anti-Semitic now, or doesn't feel that he is, but his youthful indoctrination rose up in the abandonment of his drunken state. Mel is a tortured soul because a part of him lives in a "secret" world. With the same talent he uses to create beautiful films, he created a Demon for himself that drives him to drink and cheating on his wife, family and himself. Poor, crazy, mixed up kid! Should he be pitied or kicked in the arse and taught a life lesson by losing the things he cherishes most in his life?

SIMON COWELL
LIBRA (AIR) LDN 5 (AIR)

Simon's combined natures make him a very unconventional, non-conforming free spirit. He lives in a different orbit than most persons. His Libra sign fuels his LDN 5 ruled by Mercury. If it were up to him, he would be running around the world partying most of the time. At least, he would have homes in several different countries.   He is very creative and always has new, exciting projects swimming around in his head. People like him because he is charming, although as we know, is also very out spoken. He doesn't have patience for dull, stupid or meek people. He is attracted to "ballsy", attractive, hip, creative persons like himself. As a lover, he can be super romantic and keep his lover/s quite happy. The only problem is that his LDN 5 energy induces him to change partners when he feels he is in a rut because he gets bored with the "scenario". He wants to pull the curtain down and open a new show so he can get those old feelings back that one gets when they first fall in love.

ELVIS PRESLEY
CAPRICORN (EARTH) LDN 9 (WATER)

It was known that Elvis had his dark moments in his dark bedroom. This was influenced by his Sun sign Capricorn. The God, Saturn who rules the sign Capricorn along with the same named planet was also known to take refuge in a dark, lonely place within him sometimes. Capricorns' also are known as the "Voyeurs". Often times they prefer to observe then to participate. Elvis's LDN 9 gave him the wisdom of an old spirit. He was particularly attached to his mother because he probably had a deep seeded feeling that he had been with her many times over in past lives. He was a beautiful, talented, complex man who accepted his moments of aloneness and despair and dealt with them as best he could for as long as he could. He exuded a lot of love and compassion and received the same back from his multitude of faithful fans. I hope he is happier and feels more at home now in the new world he has gone to.

JOHN LENNON
LIBRA (AIR) LDN 6 (AIR)

We all know that John was a "lovey dovey" nature and no wonder! With two Air signs both ruled by Venus, he couldn't be otherwise. He loved nurturing his children when he had the time like he did with Sean. He was always desperately seeking love and attention like all Libra number 6/s would. As Yoko grew older she wasn't into all that "koochie-koo" stuff and that was a blow to John. He felt lost and lonely without the constant displays of love and affection they had between them before. He thought of love as a "religion" and their relationship was to him, the "temple of love". He could have stayed in that mode forever. Yoko grew more realistic and let the energies of the times take her away from his "wave length". John was a true child of the 60's. He got stuck there because he felt best there and needed. to stay in that place forever even if it meant feeling lonely. Life was much more romantic and beautiful then. He played a major part in creating the love vibrations that dominated that time. When the Era began to fade, he became a saddened man with a hopeless mission as he saw his messages about love and peace fading in the minds of mankind.

NOTE FROM THE AUTHOR:

It seems that the greatest stars through time, like Elvis, John Lennon, Marilyn Monroe, Edith Piaf and Judy Garland left deep, ever lasting marks upon their fans because they exposed their inner sorrows and torment to everyone. I see it as: Above their brilliant skills, their greater talent was in arousing the deep emotions of their audience's by turning themselves inside-out to give absolutely all they possessed and all that they were. They were the living mirrors of their inner souls.

OPRAH WINFREY
AQUARIUS (AIR) LDN 4 (EARTH)

Oprah carries the Air sign of compassion combined with the very earthy LDN 4, "Big Mama" qualities. She has found great success because she has a "mission" to help people understand themselves, each other and life better so they may find more happiness. She also has the hard working LDN 4 qualities that don't give up until the job is done and done well. Other LDN 4's with different Air and not Air Sun-signs are listed below, have become the wealthiest persons' in the world. It seems to be a magical blend of energies that creates riches even though their causes or (incentives) vary. The fantasy and romantic (to them) projects that they begin for the love of dong them, turn out to be vast successes because they have the hard working, persevering nature of the LDN 4 to push them through.

DONALD TRUMP
GEMINI (AIR) LDN 4 (EARTH)

Here is an example of the same above combined energies of an Air Sun sign combined with the good, ole LDN 4. His Gemini Sun-sign makes him a bit ego-centric, eccentric, a natural flirt, and a creative "adventurer" with a need for constant changes in his life that makes an interesting contrast with his stable, steady Number 4 nature.

BILL GATES
LIBRA (AIR) LDN 4 (EARTH)

Bill is another example of the same combination of an Air Sun-sign combined with the LDN 4 becoming a super success. His Libra Sun-sign ruled by Venus gives him a more romantic and creative aspect.

As a LDN 4, he is very loving and caring of his spouse and family as well as to those who work for him. His Libra nature needs to feel harmony and balance both in his work place and at home.

RICHARD BRANSON
CANCER (WATER) LDN 4 (EARTH)

Richard is yet another example of a hard working, super successful person with the LDN 4, this time combined with a Water Sun-sign. His Cancer nature makes him the perfect family man but can also lead him into depressions at times. He feels as good on water as he does on the earth because of his combined signs. (Remember, he used to live on a boat in London's Little Italy)! He most likely did and perhaps still does his best thinking and dreaming on Water, though he needs to feel the earth beneath his feet as well, to keep him "grounded.

YOU HAVE LEARNED HOW TO CALCULATE THE LDN. YOU ALSO HAVE SEEN NUMEROUS EXAMPLES OF HOW PEOPLE CAN BE PROFILED BY THEIR LDN AND SUN-SIGNS' COMBINED. TRY OUT YOUR NEW SKILLS ON THE FOLLOWING CELEBRITIES THAT INTEREST YOU. HAVE FUN.

ADREW LLOYD WEBBER
ARIES (FIRE) LDN 2 (WATER)

BEN AFFLECK
LEO (FIRE)   LDN 6 (AIR)

NICOLLETTE SHERIDAN
SCORPIO (WATER)   LDN 6 (AIR)

JAMES BROWN
CANCER (WATER) LDN 3 (AI

KATE MOSS
CAPRICORN (EARTH) LDN 2 (WATER)

DES O'CONNOR
CAPRICORN (EARTH)   LDN 1 (FIRE)

CHRIS EVANS
CAPRICORN (EARTH) LDN 1 (FIRE)

TINA TURNER
SAGITARIUS (FIRE) LDN 5 (AIR)

KATE WINSLET
LIBRA (AIR)   LDN 1 (FIRE)

BOB DYLAN
GEMINI (AIR)   LDN 8 (FIRE)

ROD STEWART
CAPRICORN (EARTH)   LDN 3 (AIR)

RUSSELL CROWE
ARIES (FIRE)   LDN 4 (EARTH)

JACK NICHOLSON
TAURUS (EARTH) LDN 7 (AIR)

ELLE MACPHERSON
ARIES (FIRE)   LDN 7 (AIR)

SHARON STONE
PISCES (WATER)   LDN 9 (WATER)

BONO
TAURUS (EARTH)   LDN 4 (EARTH)

PAUL McCARTNEY
GEMINI (AIR)   LDN 4 (EARTH)

JAY LENO
TAURUS (EARTH)   LDN 2 (WATER)

MARGARET THATCHER
LIBRA (AIR)   LDN 5 (AIR)

SADDAM HUSSEIN
TAURUS (EARTH)   LDN 7 (AIR)

MICHAEL JORDAN
ACQUARIUS (AIR)   LDN 2 (WATER)

EDDIE MURPHY
CAPRICORN (EARTH)   LDN 5 (AIR)

ERIC CLAPTON
ARIES (FIRE)   LDN 7 (AIR

RAY CHARLES
LIBRA (AIR)   LDN 9 (WATER)

PAMELA ANDERSON
CANCER (WATER) LDN 4 (EARTH)

DIANNA ROSS
ARIES (FIRE)   LDN 2 (WATER)

DOLLY PARTON
CAPRICORN (EARTH)   LDN 4 (EARTH)

SHANIA TWAIN
VIRGO (EARTH)   LDN 3 (AIR)

LILY TOMLIN
VIRGO (EARTH)   LDN 5 (AIR)

MOHAMMED ALI
CAPRICORN (EARTH)   LDN 8 (FIRE)

EMINEM
LIBRA (AIR)   LDN 9 (WATER)

GLORIA ESTEFAN
VIRGO (EARTH)   LDN 5 (AIR)

TOMMY LEE JONES
VIRGO (EARTH)   LDN 8 (FIRE)

BRIDGET BARDOT
LIBRA (AIR)   LDN 9 (WATER)

SARAH FERGUSON
LIBRA (AIR)   LDN 4 (EARTH)

AL PACINO
TAURUS (EARTH)   LDN 7 (AIR)

REESE WITHERSPOON
ARIES (FIRE)   LDN 3 (AIR)

ARETHA FRANKLIN
ARIES (FIRE)   LDN 8 (FIRE)

RENEE ZELWEGGER
TAURUS (EARTH)   LDN 9 (WATER)

SCARLETT JOHANSSON
SCORPIO (WATER)   LDN1 (FIRE)

GERI HALIWELL
LEO (FIRE)   LDN 6 (AIR)

MARGARET THATCHER
LIBRA (AIR)   LDN 5 (AIR)

CLINT EASTWOOD
GEMINI (AIR)   LDN 4 (EARTH)

SEAN CONNERY
VIRGO (EARTH)   LDN 1 (FIRE)

www.ingramcontent.com/pod-product-compliance
Lightning Source LLC
Chambersburg PA
CBHW051956280526
45793CB00005B/742